KEMSING TUITION

11^+ PRACTICE TESTS

WITH ANSWERS AND EXPLANATIONS

Cover designed by Richard Barnes

Kemsing Tuition
Visit our website at www.kemsingtuition.co.uk

Printed in the United Kingdom

First Printing: July 2019
Kemsing Tuition Limited

ISBN 9781080113460

CONTENTS

Introduction

This book contains two complete mock tests for children who are taking the Kent Test or Eleven Plus examination. The format of the tests is similar to the actual test in the level of challenge and types of questions that may be asked.

The questions have been written by a qualified and experienced classroom teacher and private tutor. They have also been trialled with children who are getting ready for the exam and who have taken it and passed.

It is intended, unlike the real test, that the answers will be marked on the papers themselves. When they sit the real thing, answers will need to be recorded on a separate answer sheet. If this format is preferred, then a printable answer sheet can be downloaded and printed from:

www.kemsingtuition.co.uk/elevenplus2019

Full answers and explanations where useful are included at the end of the book, where you will also find advice about administering the mock tests and making sense of the results.

Kemsing Tuition is a company based in Kent which provides tuition for children and adults in a number of subjects, including preparation for entrance exams and the 11+test – please visit our website for more information if would like to know more.

MATHS

Paper 1

Instructions

1. The questions are all multiple choice – choose only one answer for each question.

2. Answer as quickly and carefully as you can. If there is a question that you cannot do, leave it and go on to the next one.

3. After two practice questions, you have **25 minutes** to complete the test.

PRACTICE QUESTIONS (5 mins)

P1. What is 3050 – 725?

A 2325 **B** 3775 **C** 1075 **D** 3025 **E** 2523

P2. I buy 5 pencils for £0.20 each and a book for £2.50 – how much do I spend altogether?

A £2.70 **B** £2.75 **C** £3.10 **D** £3.50 **E** £4.50

PLEASE WAIT UNTIL YOU ARE ASKED TO TURN OVER

1. **What is 20,009 + 7050?**

A 27,509 B 27,950 C 27,059 D 27,095 E 20,714

2. **If $\frac{3}{4}$ of a number is 60, what is $\frac{1}{10}$ of the number?**

A 80 B 8 C 6 D 45 E 4.5

3. **How many prime numbers are there between 20 and 30?**

A one B two C three D four E none

4. **What is 263 x 29?**

A 7,627 B 4,997 C 7,540 D 292 E 7,336

PLEASE TURN THE PAGE AND CONTINUE

5. **If** $a = 8,\ b = 12$ **and** $c = 15$**, what is** $c\,(2b + a)$**?**

A 1,440 **B** 300 **C** 15,248 **D** 47 **E** 480

6. **What is the area of this right-angled triangle?**

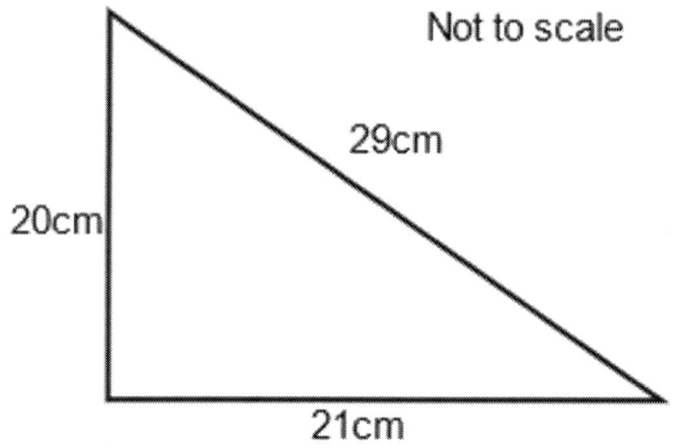

A $304.5cm^2$ **B** $210cm^2$ **C** $420cm^2$ **D** $70cm$ **E** $290cm^2$

7. **How many seconds are there in 4.25 minutes?**

A 255 **B** 240 **C** 265 **D** 10,200 **E** 425

8. A biscuit recipe requires 250g of sugar, 280g of butter, 230g of flour and 40g of cocoa powder. What fraction of the total ingredients is the sugar?

A $\frac{5}{12}$ **B** $\frac{7}{16}$ **C** $\frac{2}{9}$ **D** $\frac{5}{16}$ **E** $\frac{5}{14}$

9. The population of a country is 7,525,000. If the population density is 50 people per km^2, what is the area of the country?

A 145,000 km^2 **B** 150,500 km^2 **C** 525,000 km

D 1,505,000 km^2 **E** 7,525,000 km^2

10. What is 20.06 + 7.9 + 105.003?

A 132.18 **B** 133.8 **C** 132.936 **D** 132.963 **E** 130.15

PLEASE TURN THE PAGE AND CONTINUE

11. The pie chart below shows the favourite sports of Year 5 at Pinnacle Primary School. If 12 children chose cricket, how many children are there in the whole year group?

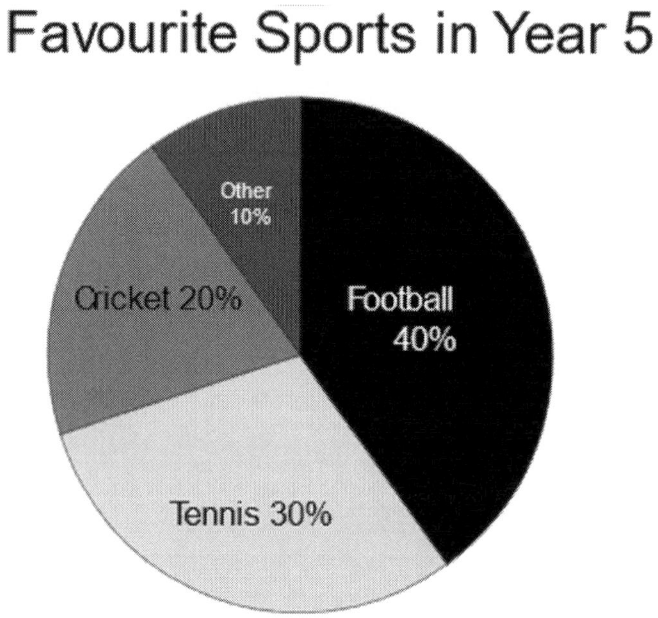

A 30 **B** 40 **C** 50 **D** 60 **E** 70

12. Oli does a paper round from Monday – Friday, delivering 165 papers each day. He gets paid £0.07 for each paper he delivers. How much does he earn per week?

A £57.75 **B** £115.50 **C** £1,155.00 **D** £5,775.00 **E** £577.50

13. **Eight students scored these marks on a test. What is the range of these marks?**

75, 69, 82, 67, 79, 70, 84, 82

A 17 **B** 18 **C** 82 **D** 8 **E** 76

14. **Look at the line graph below which shows Dave's cycling journey. For how long did he stop for lunch?**

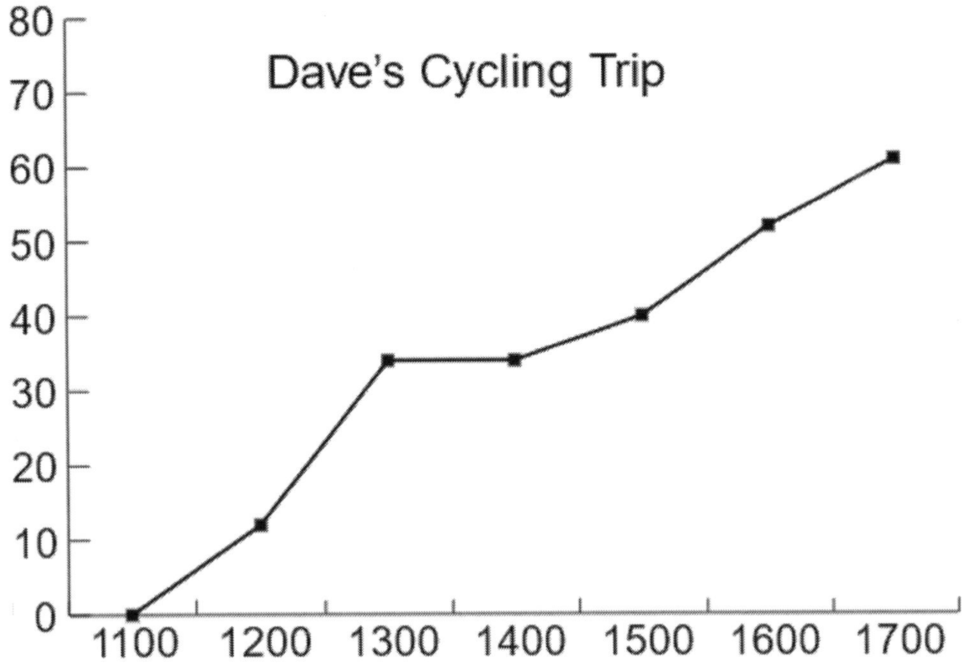

A 1200 **B** 45 mins **C** 1 hour **D** 8 hours **E** noon

PLEASE TURN THE PAGE AND CONTINUE

15. **I think of a number, multiply it by 8, add 23 and then double it. The answer is 78. What number did I think of?**

A 2 **B** 5 **C** 189 **D** 7 **E** 23

16. **How many millimetres are there in half a km?**

A 500 B 5,000 C 50,000 D 500,000 E 5 million

17. **What is the next number in this sequence?**

7, 9, 13, 21, 37, 69, ……

A 71 B 73 C 138 D 133 E 106

18. **In London, the temperature is 23° but in Reykjavik, the temperature is -7°. What is the difference in temperature between the two places?**

A 16° **B** 30° **C** 17° **D** 40° **E** 18°

19. What number is halfway between 12 and 19?

A 13 **B** 14.5 **C** 15 **D** 15.5 **E** 16

20. What percentage of this shape is shaded?

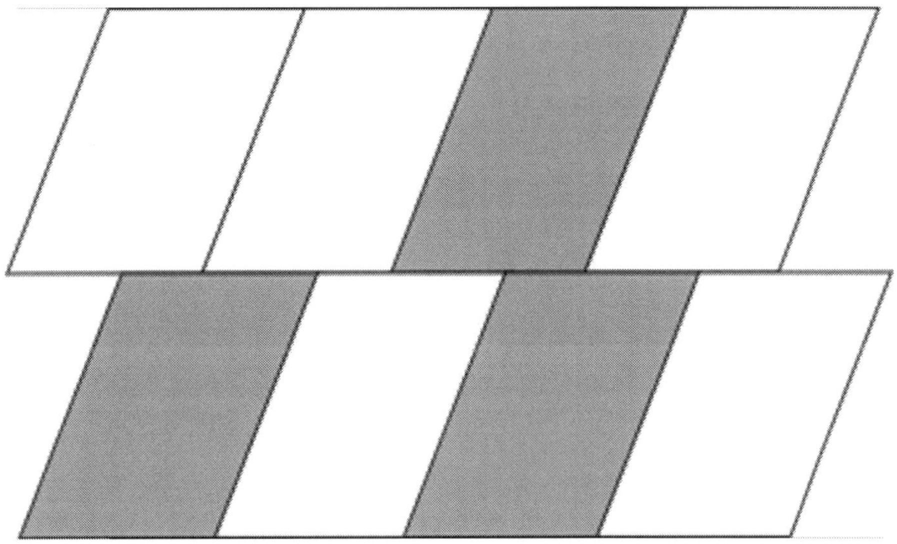

A 15% **B** 25% **C** 37.5% **D** 40% **E** 45%

PLEASE TURN THE PAGE AND CONTINUE

21. Bob earns £12,500 a year. He receives a pay rise of 2.5%. How much does he earn now?

A £12,800.90 B £12,750.20 C £12,812.50
D £12,502.50 E £12, 525.00

22. The number of ants in a colony doubles every 10 days. On 20th April, there are 240 ants.

On what date will there be 960 ants?

A 30th April B 10th May C 17th May D 20th May E 30th May

23. Which of these numbers is NOT a square number, a cube number or a prime number?

A 5 B 25 C 125 D 216 E 250

24. Jasper's swimming lesson begins at 2.30pm.

He needs 15 minutes to get changed and 35 minutes to travel to the pool.

What is the latest time that he should leave home so that he doesn't miss his lesson?

A 13:30 **B** 13:40 **C** 13:50 **D** 13:55 **E** 14:15

25. What is 90% of £12.00?

A £9.00 **B** £9.60 **C** £10.80 **D** £11.00 **E** £21.00

THE MATHS SECTION OF THE TEST IS COMPLETE
NOW CHECK YOUR ANSWERS

PLEASE WAIT UNTIL YOU ARE ASKED
TO TURN OVER

ENGLISH

Paper 1

Instructions

1. The questions are all multiple choice – choose only one answer for each question.

2. You have to read a passage and answer questions about it, as well as some additional questions about spelling, punctuation and grammar. You can look back at the passage as many times as you want.

3. Answer as quickly and carefully as you can. If there is a question that you cannot do, leave it and go on to the next one.

4. After two practice questions, you have **25 minutes** to complete the test.

PRACTICE QUESTIONS (5 mins)

P1. Which of these words is an adjective?

A happily **B** cold **C** trumpet **D** because **E** me

The correct answer is **B** cold as it could describe a noun.

P2. How many spelling mistakes are there in the following sentence?

I waited pateintly for the expres train to arrive at the station, but I dydn't want to be late for my appointment.

A one **B** two **C** three **D** four **E** five

The correct answer is **C** three spelling mistakes:

patiently,
express *and*
didn't

PLEASE WAIT UNTIL YOU ARE ASKED TO TURN OVER

Read the following passage carefully and then answer the questions that follow:

Extract from "The Eponymic Sock Monster" by Marie-Anne Pinkney

Marie-Anne did not want to get up. Getting up was awful for three main reasons: it was too cold and it was much nicer to just stay curled up under a warm duvet, it was too dark (who wants to get up in the middle of the night) and it was too...

Perhaps more time was needed to think of what the third one would be, but there had to be one and if anyone could find it, Marie-Anne could because she was clever. Not just a little bit above average, but approaching genius level, or so she believed after her teacher told her that she had an IQ of a million. The only possible way to beat that would be to have an IQ of a googol (the digit one followed by a hundred zeros) and Marie-Anne didn't think that was even possible.

A bell rang.

This was the breakfast bell and was mum's signal to the rest of the household that the porridge was nearly cooked and that it would very soon be arriving on the dining table. This was all very exciting if you were up and dressed and hungry but whilst still in bed it was a warning of the dire consequences of not being at the table on time and missing breakfast altogether. This was not an idle threat; Marie-Anne had missed breakfast completely on at least five occasions so far and considering that she was only nine years old, that was quite a lot.

So, a decision had to be made: jump out of bed, get dressed as fast as a rocket, rush downstairs and sit at the table just in time to gulp down the whole bowl of hot porridge in under a minute, or stay in bed a bit longer, then get dressed as fast as a rocket, rush downstairs, sit at the table, be told that it was too late to have breakfast, scream and cry and then get dragged to school feeling very hungry.

Marie-Anne pondered those two choices for too long because the latter is what actually happened (mostly). The only difference was that mum decided to leave to take the other children to school and to abandon Marie-Anne in the house on her own in order to make her own way to school, which was three miles away.

That is why Marie-Anne was sitting on the stairs, hungry and tearful and slightly worried about what to do next. That is when she had a very clever and brilliant idea and was absolutely sure that her IQ was extremely high indeed.

Marie-Anne's idea was, by even her own high standards, brilliantly amazingly fantastic and this was it:

Firstly, she would leave a note for her mum (who undoubtedly would return sooner or later) with a nonsensical explanation for why she wasn't there (this would require a little further thought).

Secondly, she would hide somewhere that her mum would not think of looking (this too would require further thought).

Thirdly, she would wait long enough for her mum to be a little bit worried but not too worried and not worried enough to call the police. If that happened, then the plan would have gone very wrong.

This was clearly a plan with upsides and downsides, but then isn't every plan like that, even those devised by geniuses?

So to put the plan into action... Marie-Anne dashed around the house to find some notepaper (she found some that had cute giraffes in the corner), a pen (she actually found two but one of them didn't work) and started to write:

"Dear mum,

I am sad that you went without me. I am now going to find..."

Marie-Anne paused. It had to be a credible threat but at the same time not too credible. She remembered something that mum had said to her the night before when she couldn't understand why it was impossible to match a pair of socks when sorting out the laundry. For some unbeknownst reason, socks constantly disappeared without trace and no-one found them again. Mum didn't have a good explanation for this other than someone must have been stealing them or something. The entity that was blamed for the whole situation was called...

"the sock monster" (credible threat, not too credible) and so that is how the note was completed. And as mum would not know where the Sock Monster lived, she wouldn't come looking and then after a short while (according to the plan), her lost daughter would reappear, be given some late breakfast and all would be well.

Having decided to hide somewhere, pretending to be in the presence of a sock monster, Marie-Anne needed to think of the perfect hiding place.

But where? Three suitable places came to mind: firstly, there was a small cupboard upstairs that she passed every morning on the way to the bathroom. No-one seemed to go in there, except for when they needed something exotic such as multicoloured glitter. However, this cupboard was kept locked all of the time so unless she could find a key, it would be unsuitable.

The second hiding place that Marie-Anne thought of was the downstairs cupboard, under the stairs. This was where everyone kept their coats and a vacuum cleaner lived there as well. It was never locked, but there was a high probability that this would be the first place for her mum to look so this option seemed rather risky.

Marie-Anne's third idea was (like baby bear's porridge in the story of Goldilocks) just right – unlikely for mum to look there and no locked door, and this was the garden shed at the bottom of the garden. In fact, Marie-Anne, although she had looked in the shed a few times, had never actually been in there and so wasn't entirely sure what was stored in there. The door was definitely not locked though, and it would be nice and cosy.

So, down the long garden path Marie-Anne sauntered, checking over her shoulder a few times to see if her mum had returned (which she hadn't) and opened the door.

The door made a terrible squeaking noise when it opened but once inside, with the door shut behind her, it was time to settle in. Pulling a long string made a dim light come on in the centre of the shed roof and by closing the blind covering the single window, Marie-Anne felt safe and undiscoverable and sat on the wooden floor to think.

YOU MAY NOW BEGIN ANSWERING THE QUESTIONS

YOU MAY REFER BACK TO THE PASSAGE AS MANY TIMES AS YOU WANT TO

1. How many reasons did Marie-Anne *actually* give for not wanting to get up?

A none
B one
C two
D three
E four

2. On line 8, the following is an example of what?

(the digit one followed by a hundred zeros)

A hyperbole
B parentheses
C stanza
D paragraph
E contradiction

3. Which of these is closest in meaning of *dire consequences* on line 14?

A bad omens
B terrible thing that will happen
C special
D alarm bells
E awful things that have been

PLEASE TURN THE PAGE AND CONTINUE

4. How did mum let the rest of the family know that it was time for breakfast?

A rang a bell
B shouted up the stairs
C made the porridge
D expected everyone on time
E sent a message

5. What does the word *idle* mean as used on line 15?

A lazy
B empty
C silly
D unusual
E mystery

6. Which of these words is the opposite of *pondered* on line 23?

A considered
B resumed
C waterfall
D lost
E neglected

7. The explanation that Marie-Anne writes on the note is described as being...

A nonsense
B sensible
C variable
D temporary
E cautious

8. How would Marie-Anne know if her plan had gone wrong?

A her mum came back unexpectedly
B she got eaten by a monster
C the police would have been called
D her mum would have worried
E her mum would find her

9. In the paragraph that begins on line 47 and ends on line 53, which word means *being*?

A unbeknownst
B entity
C credible
D trace
E situation

PLEASE TURN THE PAGE AND CONTINUE

10. The whole passage implies that Marie-Anne is...

A decisive
B amazing
C immodest
D spiteful
E deluded

11. Which of these is an example of a *simile*?

A *like baby bear's porridge*
B *she was only nine years old*
C *be given some late breakfast*
D *as mum would not know*
E *so this option seemed rather risky*

12. How does Marie-Anne proceed down the garden path towards the shed?

A rambles
B darts
C sneaks
D ambles
E journeys

The next five questions are about spelling. Read the sentence and locate the spelling error.

Circle the letter below the error or circle N if there isn't one.

13. The garden consisted of rhododendrons, gladioli and daisys.

A B C D E N

14. Presumabely, the shed would not contain agricultural equipment or

A B C

mechanical devices.

D E N

15. This escapade would have to be mentioned in future correspondence.

A B C D E N

16. Materials such as would and glass can be utilised to construct outbuildings.

A B C D E N

17. Adventures similer to this were a regular feature of her daughter's life.

A B C D E N

PLEASE TURN THE PAGE AND CONTINUE

The next five questions are about punctuation. Locate the punctuation error on each line and circle the letter nearest to the error.

Circle N if there isn't one.

Consider the five lines to be all one paragraph.

18. All of the shelves, in the wooden shed seemed very

A B C D E N

19. neatly arranged this was unexpected, as she

A B C D E N

20. knew that her dad was not a tidy person: and this

A B C D E N

21. was *his* shed, so why would mum

A B C D E N

22. practise her organisational skills in here.

A B C D E N

For the next eight questions, choose the best word or phrase to fit in the gap.

23. To pass the time, Marie-Anne mentally _______ the stored items.

A started
B moved
C lost
D catalogued
E saw

24. She _____________ more bemused as she compared what she saw to her idea of what things should be kept in a shed.

A is
B answered
C became
D silently
E came

25. On the highest shelf on the left was a _______ of neatly arranged books.

A row
B argument
C shelf
D librarian
E ordering

PLEASE TURN THE PAGE AND CONTINUE

26. They must have been in a foreign language as Marie-Anne did not recognise a single word on _______ spines.

A there
B their
C these
D this
E them

27. Next to those, in the _______ centre of the highest shelf, was a small lamp with a purple lampshade which appeared to have a wire that vanished out of sight and may have been plugged in somewhere.

A main
B precious
C total
D middle
E exact

28. To the far right of the high shelf was a pile of clothes, about the right size for someone her brother's age (________________) and mostly in bright colours.

A her brother Tim
B six and a half
C a huge stack
D very tall
E made her cry

29. She didn't remember ever seeing her brother wearing clothes resembling these ones and she certainly had never, ________________, worn them.

A as her brother
B she went outside
C never is a long time
D even though
E to her knowledge

PLEASE TURN THE PAGE AND CONTINUE

30. A second, lower-down shelf, had equally _______________ objects: a stack of white plates, a cardboard box labelled in the same foreign language as the books above, a cuddly fish, a stack of three plastic boxes which contained something resembling sandwiches and a large plant pot. Well at least the plant pot belongs here, Marie-Anne thought.

A incongruous
B inconceivable
C in her dreams
D innovative
E in the midst of confusion

THE ENGLISH SECTION OF THE TEST IS COMPLETE

PLEASE DO NOT TURN THE PAGE

VERBAL REASONING

Paper 1

1. Read the instructions carefully for each set of questions.
2. You can continue until the end of the test.
3. You do not need to wait for further instructions once you have started.

DO NOT TURN THE PAGE UNTIL YOU ARE ASKED TO BEGIN

Section 1

Find two words, one from each group which are most <u>opposite</u> in meaning.

Circle both answers.

Example:

(hot hill hind) (back mountain cold)

(A) hot	**X** back
B hill	**Y** mountain
C hind	**(Z)** cold

The correct answers are **A** and **Z** as hot and cold are opposite in meaning.

NOW TURN THE PAGE AND COMPLETE THE QUESTIONS IN THIS SECTION

1. (alert consent warm) (tepid warn agree)

A alert
B consent
C warm

X tepid
Y negligent
Z agree

2. (hinder medicate bruise) (tender heal endure)

A hinder
B medicate
C bruise

X tender
Y heal
Z endure

3. (superfluous fluid needed) (lesser vial vital)

A superfluous
B fluid
C needed

X lesser
Y vial
Z vital

4. (dispense disappear detain) (arrive keep vanish)

A dispense
B disappear
C detain

X arrive
Y keep
Z vanish

5. (river unorthodox mate) (canal ally mainstream)

A river
B unorthodox
C mate

X canal
Y ally
Z mainstream

6. (cease debate uniform) (even argue inaugurate)

A cease	**X** even
B debate	**Y** argue
C uniform	**Z** inaugurate

7. (succumb sit failure) (yield withstand satisfy)

A succumb	**X** yield
B sit	**Y** withstand
C failure	**Z** satisfy

NOW CONTINUE WITH SECTION 2

YOU DO NOT NEED TO WAIT FOR FURTHER INSTRUCTIONS

PLEASE TURN THE PAGE AND CONTINUE

Section 2

In this section, find a four-letter word hidden at the end of one word and the beginning of another. Choose the option that contains the pair of words hiding the four-letter word.

Example:

The man eats breakfast in the morning.

A The man
(**B**) man eats
C eats breakfast
D breakfast in
E the morning

The correct answer is **B** man eats, as this contains the hidden word *neat*.

NOW COMPLETE THE QUESTIONS IN THIS SECTION

8. Have you considered items other than those?

A you considered

B considered items

C items other

D other than

E than those

9. Leave illegal goods behind and never return

A Leave illegal

B illegal goods

C goods behind

D and never

E never return

10. Presumably its pancake got eaten immediately and without incident.

A Presumably its

B its pancake

C pancake got

D eaten immediately

E without incident

PLEASE TURN THE PAGE AND CONTINUE

11. **Don't forget to commence the spin to enable the machine to work correctly.**

A forget to
B to commence
C the spin
D spin to
E machine to

12. **Where is the protagonist, the one who offered to vindicate their step-brother?**

A the protagonist
B one who
C who offered
D vindicate their
E their step-brother

13. **Innocuous comments are hardly related to anything mean or disputatious.**

A comments are
B hardly related
C anything mean
D or disputatious
E Innocuous comments

14. **Veiled criticism, ugly and pretentious, does sometimes produce consistency.**

A criticism ugly

B ugly and

C pretentious does

D does sometimes

E produce consistency

15. **Lifeless analogue cars Americans drive don't necessarily work.**

A Lifeless analogue

B analogue cars

C cars Americans

D Americans drive

E necessarily work

PLEASE TURN THE PAGE AND ANSWER QUESTION 16

16. Read the following information, then find the correct answer from the options below.

Dave plays the saxophone. He practises for ninety minutes each weekday (apart from Tuesday when he has his lesson) and for two hours every weekend (either on Saturday or Sunday but never both).

Today is Monday 3rd July and his saxophone exam is on the 10th July . If he is able to practise today, but not on the day of his exam, how many hours of practice will he be able to do before his exam?

A six hours
B seven and a half hours
C eight hours
D nine hours
E nine and a half hours

NOW CONTINUE WITH SECTION 3
YOU DO NOT NEED TO WAIT FOR FURTHER INSTRUCTIONS

Section 3

In each question, work out the missing number indicated by the question mark and select the correct answer from the options given.

Example:

3 6 9 [?] 15 18

A 10 **B** 11 **(C)** 12 **D** 13 **E** 14

The correct answer is **C** as the numbers are going up in threes.

NOW TURN THE PAGE AND COMPLETE THE QUESTIONS IN THIS SECTION

17. 28 32 37 [?] 50 58

A 40 B 41 C 42 D 43 E 44

18. 4 8 12 20 [?] 52 84

A 32 B 42 C 28 D 38 E 48

19. 100 [?] 64 49 36 25

A 121 B 81 C 101 D 71 E 91

20. 2 4 12 48 [?]

A 96 B 16 C 192 D 240 E 480

21. [?] 100 95 92.5 91.25

A 210 B 110 C 105 D 102.5 E 105.5

22. 2 4 8 [?] 32 64

A 12 B 16 C 20 D 28 E 30

23. 142 252 362 472 [?]

A 362 B 562 C 482 D 572 E 582

24. 291 [?] 306 321 341 366

A 299 B 296 C 300 D 302 E 292

PLEASE TURN THE PAGE AND CONTINUE

25. **11 111 161 186 [?]**

A 196 **B** 211 **C** 198.5 **D** 286 **E** 200

26. **[?] 3 12 60 360**

A 0 **B** 1 **C** 2 **D** 3 **E** 4

27. **6 12 12 24 [?] 36**

A 26 **B** 18 **C** 20 **D** 32 **E** 40

NOW CONTINUE WITH SECTION 4

YOU DO NOT NEED TO WAIT FOR FURTHER INSTRUCTIONS

Section 4

Use the alphabet to help you find the next pair of letters in the sequence.

A B C D E F G H I J K L M N O P Q R S T U V W X Y Z

Example:

AB	**BC**	**CD**	**DE**	**[?]**
(**A**) EF	**B** FF	**C** FG	**D** CG	**E** EH

The correct answer is **A**

The first and second letters in each pair go up by one letter each time and so the next letters are E and F.

NOW TURN THE PAGE AND COMPLETE THE QUESTIONS IN THIS SECTION

A B C D E F G H I J K L M N O P Q R S T U V W X Y Z

28. HJ LN PR TV [?]

A XY **B** XZ **C** WY **D** TX **E** ZX

29. CY FV IS LP [?]

A OQ **B** PS **C** QS **D** OM **E** QM

30. CE EH HL LQ [?]

A QV **B** PV **C** PQ **D** QP **E** QW

31. BY DV FS HP [?]

A JS **B** JR **C** IT **D** JM **E** JY

32. AX BZ DC GG [?]

A JL **B** JM **C** HH **D** MJ **E** KL

A B C D E F G H I J K L M N O P Q R S T U V W X Y Z

33. CC BE AG ZI [?]

A XC **B** YK **C** ZE **D** XD **E** ZC

34. HK MF RA WV [?]

A BB **B** CQ **C** BQ **D** CD **E** CB

35. AP ZD BO YE [?]

A YF **B** CN **C** ZX **D** RE **E** XA

36. TA SF QJ NM [?]

A NO **B** SO **C** TO **D** MO **E** JO

NOW CONTINUE WITH SECTION 5

YOU DO <u>NOT</u> NEED TO WAIT FOR FURTHER INSTRUCTIONS

PLEASE TURN THE PAGE AND CONTINUE

Section 5

In these questions, the same letter must fit into both sets of brackets to create four correctly spelt words.

Example:

lan [?] ate　　　**pon [?] art**

A p　　　(**B**) d　　　**C** e　　　**D** y　　　**E** s

The correct answer is **B** as the letter d makes four words:

land,
date,
pond *and*
dart

NOW COMPLETE THE QUESTIONS IN THIS SECTION

37. **pla [?] ear** **sta [?] ard**

A n **B** t **C** y **D** b **E** d

38. **foi [?] isp** **hur [?] ute**

A l **B** d **C** m **D** n **E** w

39. **gna [?] ane** **fle [?] ine**

A t **B** p **C** w **D** d **E** e

40. **tru [?] ver** **tre [?] asy**

A d **B** o **C** p **D** f **E** e

41. **van [?] ast** **con [?] dge**

A s **B** e **C** t **D** n **E** p

PLEASE TURN THE PAGE AND CONTINUE

42. pos [?] ail   bat [?] oax

A h   **B** t   **C** c   **D** s   **E** e

43. fra [?] our   all [?] oke

A t   **B** o   **C** g   **D** y   **E** s

44. num [?] ile   com [?] rie

A o   **B** p   **C** s   **D** b   **E** u

NOW CONTINUE WITH SECTION 6

YOU DO NOT NEED TO WAIT FOR FURTHER INSTRUCTIONS

Section 6

Which word goes equally well with both pairs of words?

Example:

(alto, soprano)   (plaice, cod)

(**A**) bass   **B** tenor   **C** fish   **D** location   **E** gold

The correct answer is **A** bass.
A bass can be a singer (to go with alto and soprano)
and can be a fish (to go with plaice and cod)

NOW TURN THE PAGE AND COMPLETE THE QUESTIONS IN THIS SECTION

45. (happy, gratified) (constitution, capacity)

A gleeful **B** measure **C** content **D** great **E** document

46. (punishment, reward) (abandon, abscond)

A prize **B** quit **C** freedom **D** desert **E** vacate

47. (litter, junk) (disobey, ignore)

A refuse **B** mess **C** condone **D** blank **E** condemn

48. (gust, squall) (twist, meander)

A tornado **B** turn **C** breeze **D** curved **E** wind

49. **(microscopic, insignificant) (jiffy, flash)**

A detailed **B** minute **C** cursory **D** moment **E** precise

50. **(scheme, venture) (impel, cast)**

A project **B** develop **C** distend **D** shoot **E** task

51. **(multifaceted, complex) (amalgam, combination)**

A multipart **B** multifarious **C** mixture

D multiple **E** compound

PLEASE TURN THE PAGE AND ANSWER QUESTION 52

52. Read the information below and then answer the question that follows:

Zeon has to be at his job interview at precisely 1435. To get there, he must take a 45 minute train journey. It takes him 10 minutes to walk to the station from his house and 20 minutes to walk from the station at his destination to the interview.

At what time should he set off from home in order to be at the job interview on time, assuming that he needs to be at the station 5 minutes before the train arrives?

A 1.20 p.m.
B 11.30 a.m.
C 1.15 p.m.
D 11.55 a.m.
E 1.20 a.m.

NOW CONTINUE WITH SECTION 7
YOU DO NOT NEED TO WAIT FOR FURTHER INSTRUCTIONS

Section 7

The word in capitals has three consecutive letters removed.

These letters make one correctly spelt word, without changing their order.

The sentence must make sense. Select the correct three letter word from the options given.

Example:

The girl **PDED** to go to the party.

A AND **B** LEA **C** END **D** ICE **E** ODD

The correct answer is **B** LEA
The girl **PLEADED** to go to the party.

NOW TURN THE PAGE AND COMPLETE THE QUESTIONS IN THIS SECTION

53. The teacher said that her results were INCONSIST.

A ANT **B** SIT **C** IRE **D** ONE **E** TEN

54. How much ice cream did you **CONE** at the party?

A DON **B** RID **C** SUM **D** LED **E** TEE

55. The village consisted of over a thousand **INHAANTS**.

A BIT **B** BAT **C** ERR **D** ORE **E** BET

56. The **MAY** was so serious that she had to go to hospital for treatment.

A ILL **B** AND **C** LAY **D** ARE **E** LAD

57. The **PREIOUS** building could fall down at any moment and so no-one was allowed near it.

A VAT **B** CAN **C** SUN **D** CAR **E** MID

58. I had to **SP** down low so that I didn't hit my head on the low ceiling.

A OON **B** TOO **C** COO **D** AID **E** CAR

59. The Prime Minister asked the Queen to **SUSD** parliament.

A OUR **B** AID **C** PEN **D** TON **E** POT

60. Despite using a copious amount of glue, the two pieces would still not **ADE** together.

A SIP **B** HAT **C** LED **D** VAN **E** HER

61. The butcher gave me a **VAT** look when I asked for a loaf of bread.

A SIR **B** CAN **C** IDE **D** TAT **E** KEN

NOW CONTINUE WITH SECTION 8

YOU DO NOT NEED TO WAIT FOR FURTHER INSTRUCTIONS

PLEASE TURN THE PAGE AND CONTINUE

Section 8

Choose one word from each group which make a new word when they are put together.

The word from the first group always comes first.

Circle both answers.

Example:

(**A**) whole	**X** heart
B tired	**Y** thing
C strain	(**Z**) some

The correct answers are **A** and **Z** as
whole+some = wholesome

NOW COMPLETE THE QUESTIONS IN THIS SECTION

62.

A this **X** thing
B no **Y** gate
C watch **Z** time

63.

A intent **X** full
B rest **Y** train
C waste **Z** ion

64.

A home **X** goat
B silly **Y** ward
C scrape **Z** season

65.

A night **X** stars
B honey **Y** sun
C hot **Z** dew

PLEASE TURN THE PAGE AND CONTINUE

66.

A up
B down
C under

X of
Y in
Z on

67.

A hers
B his
C their

X elf
Y one
Z and

68.

A less
B pass
C form

X at
Y eat
Z sure

69.

A rise
B pins
C pan

X let
Y eat
Z tripe

NOW CONTINUE WITH SECTION 9
YOU DO NOT NEED TO WAIT FOR FURTHER INSTRUCTIONS

Section 9

Use the alphabet to solve these codes.

A B C D E F G H I J K L M N O P Q R S T U V W X Y Z

Example:

If the code for **PLACE** is **OKZBD**, which of these is the code for **HOUSE**?

A GNTRD **B** AGHRS **C** MKIUY **D** POSWL **E** OJOLL

The correct answer is **A** GNTRD

Each letter in the word is changed to the letter that comes before it in the code:

NOW TURN THE PAGE AND COMPLETE THE QUESTIONS IN THIS SECTION

A B C D E F G H I J K L M N O P Q R S T U V W X Y Z

70. If the code for **CRATER** is **ETCVGT**, which of these is the code for **MOON**?

A KMML **B** OQQP **C** LNNM **D** VFFG **E** RSSU

71. If the code for **RANDOM** is **QYKZJG**, which of these is the code for **NUMBER**?

A NMJXLZ **B** MSXJQR **C** MNPQJS **D** MXZLJH **E** MSJXZL

72. If the code for **BISCUIT** is **&*£%!*@**, which of these is the code for **SUITABLE**?

A $!*%+*=# **B** @&!*+&=# **C** £!*@+&=#

D *&%$+@=# **E** £*!$+&=#

A B C D E F G H I J K L M N O P Q R S T U V W X Y Z

73. If the code for **RISEN** is **WnXjS**, which of these is the code for **SPOON**?

A XUttS **B** UXttY **C** opMMg **D** paYYz **E** LWssH

74. If the code for **CREATE** is **395262022**, which word does the code 1826202219 represent?

A RITES **B** RATES **C** RIOTS **D** RISES **E** RELAY

NOW CONTINUE WITH SECTION 10

YOU DO NOT NEED TO WAIT FOR FURTHER INSTRUCTIONS

PLEASE TURN THE PAGE AND CONTINUE

Section 10

Use the information to solve each sum. Select the letter that represents the answer.

Example:

A = 16 B = 5 C = 14 (D)= 6 E = 8

(A + C) ÷ B = ?

The correct answer is **D**
(16 + 14) ÷ 5 = 30 ÷ 5 = 6

NOW COMPLETE THE QUESTIONS IN THIS SECTION

75.

A = 4 **B** = 27 **C** = 12 **D** = 9 **E** = 24

D (C ÷ A) = ?

76.

A = 5 **B** = 2 **C** = 13 **D** = 14 **E** = 3

D ÷ (C – EB) = ?

77.

A = 2 **B** = 4 **C** = 6 **D** = 8 **E** = 10

A (A + A^2 + B – C)= ?

PLEASE TURN THE PAGE AND CONTINUE

78.

A = $\frac{1}{2}$ **B** = $\frac{1}{4}$ **C** = $\frac{3}{4}$ **D** = 3 **E** = 1

(A + B + C) ÷ DE = ?

79.

A = 7 **B** = 100 **C** = 84 **D** = 8 **E** = 0.5

B – C ÷ A ÷ E + D = ?

80.

A = 11 **B** = 110 **C** = 0 **D** = 99 **E** = 89

(D – D)(AE + BD + ED) = ?

THE VERBAL REASONING TEST IS COMPLETE

PLEASE DO <u>NOT</u> TURN THE PAGE

NON-VERBAL REASONING

Paper 1

Instructions

1. The questions are all multiple choice – choose only one answer for each question.

2. Answer as quickly and carefully as you can. If there is a question that you cannot do, leave it and go on to the next one.

3. You will be given instructions about each section and the amount of time you have to complete it in addition to working through an example question.

Section 1 (Time allowed - 6 minutes)

For the next twelve questions, decide which picture belongs with the group above it. Circle the correct letter.

Example:

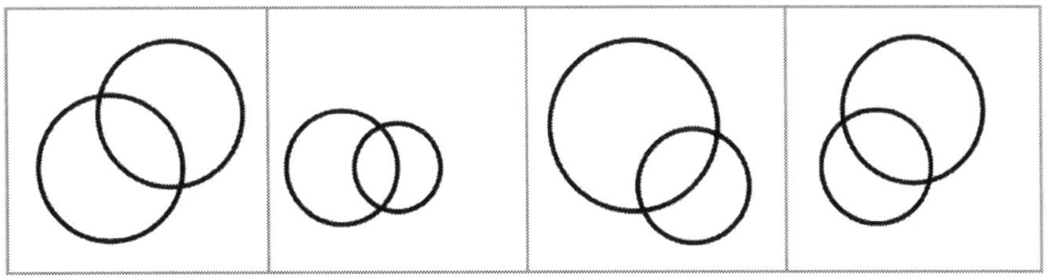

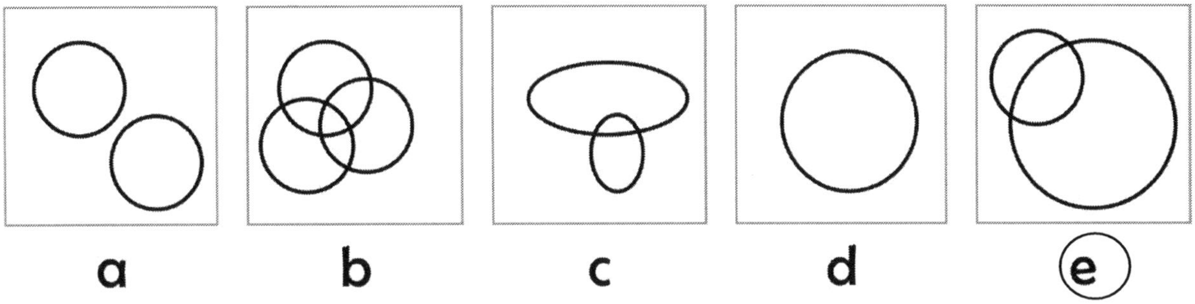

The correct answer is: **e**

The picture should have two circles overlapping.

PLEASE WAIT UNTIL YOU ARE ASKED TO TURN OVER

1.

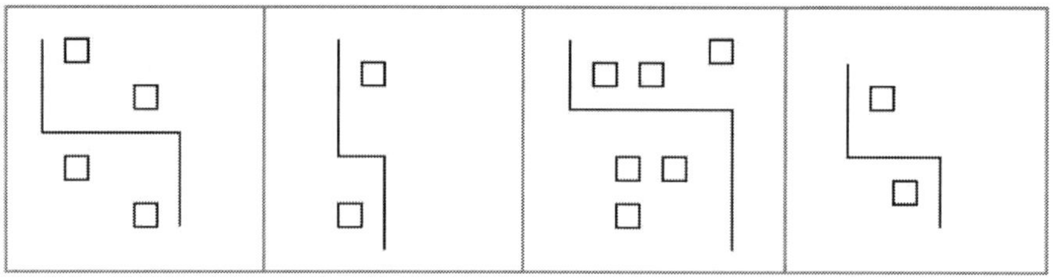

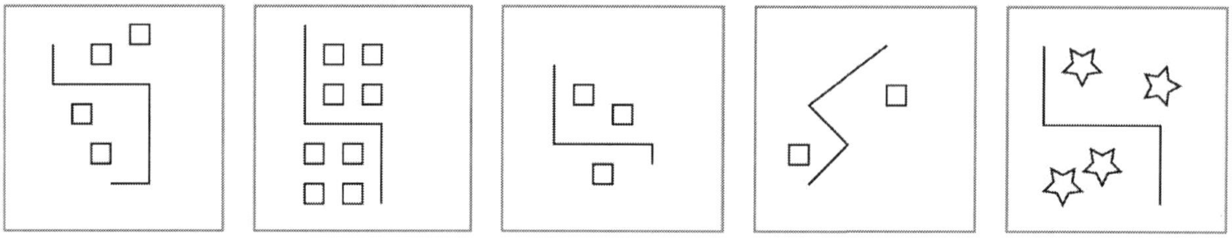

a b c d e

2.

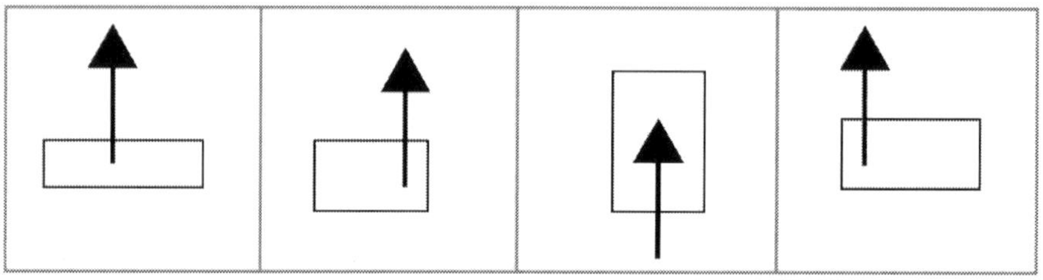

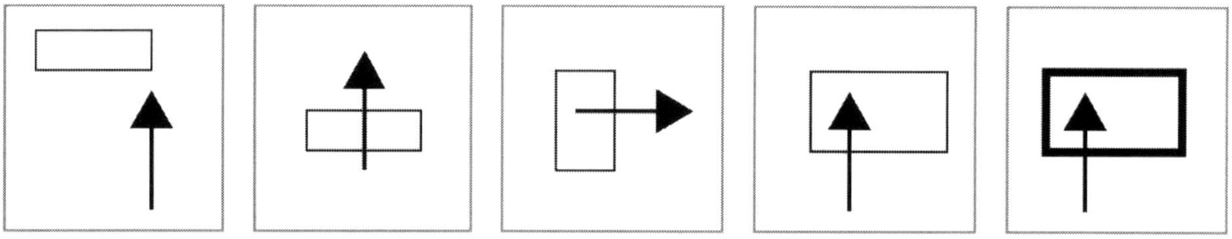

a b c d e

3.

a b c d e

4.

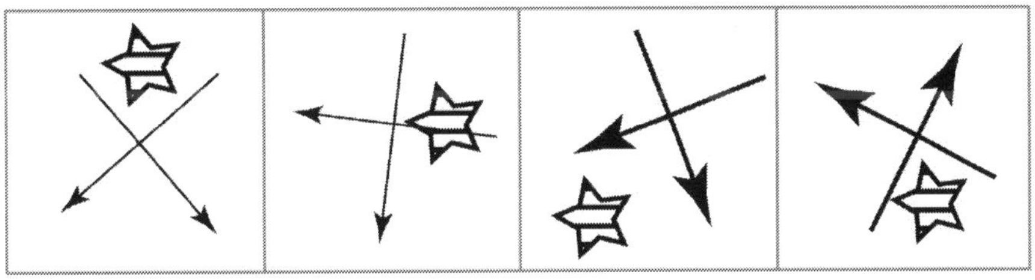

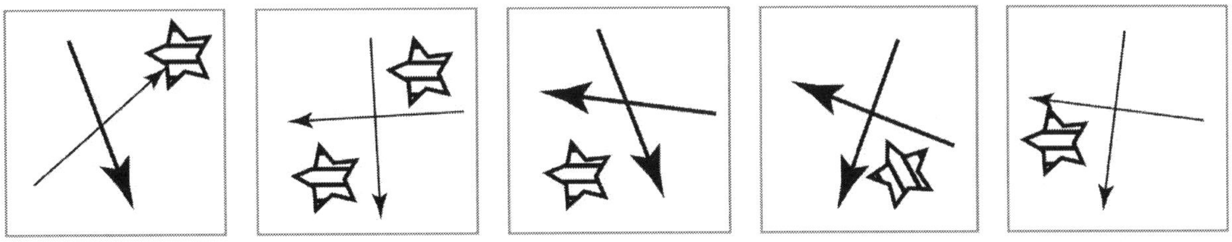

a b c d e

PLEASE TURN THE PAGE AND CONTINUE

5.

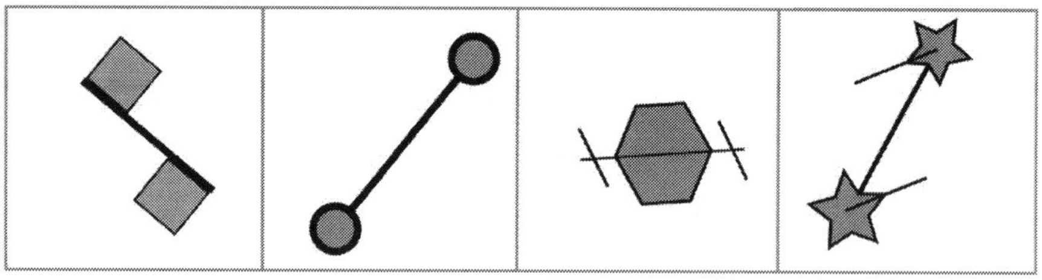

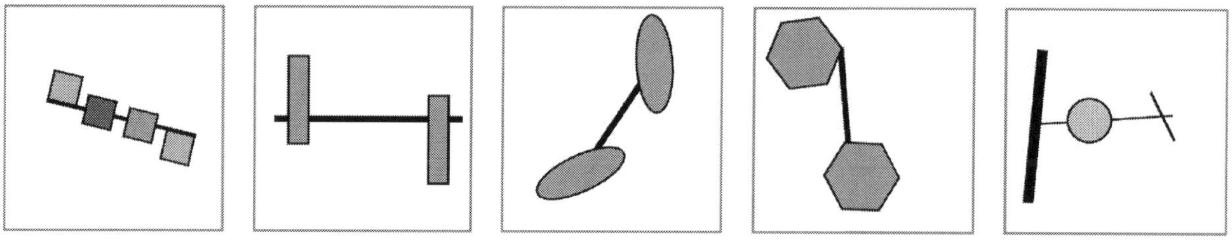

a b c d e

6.

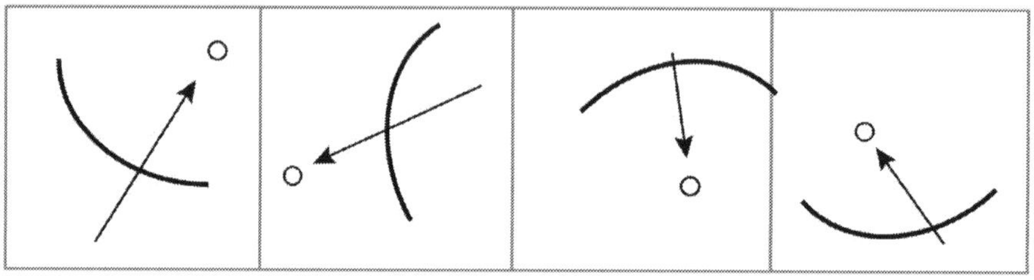

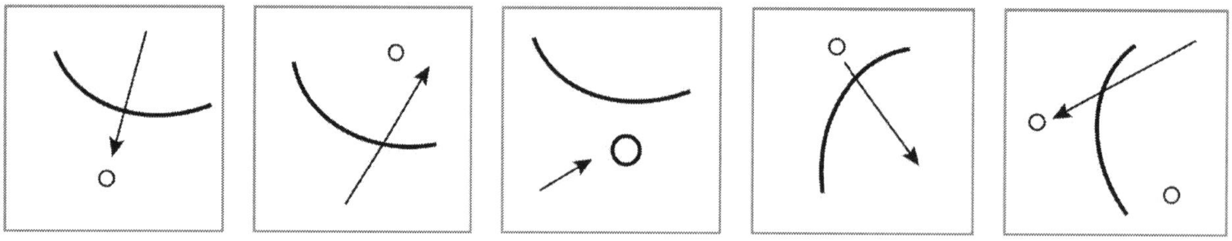

a b c d e

7.

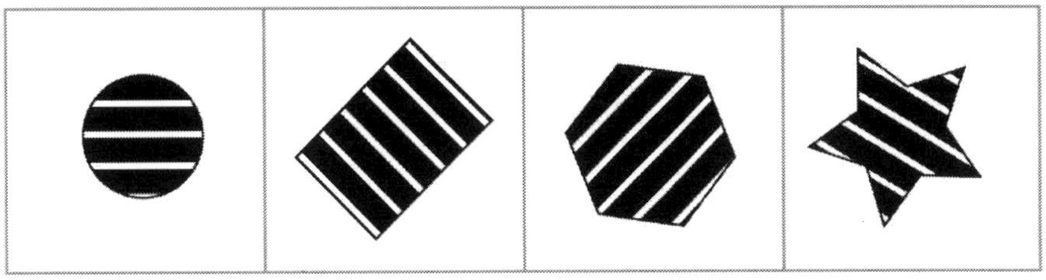

a b c d e

8.

a b c d e

PLEASE TURN THE PAGE AND CONTINUE

9.

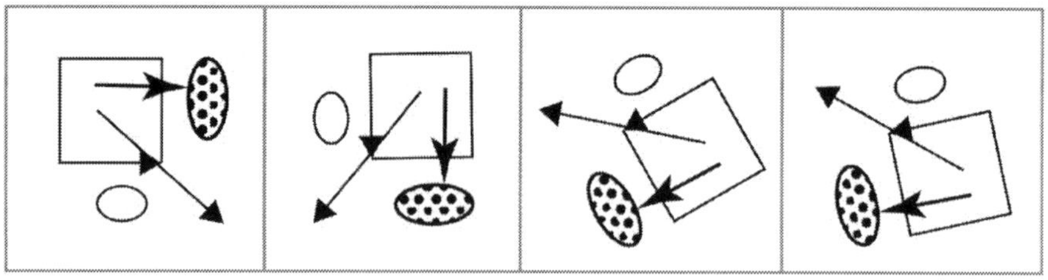

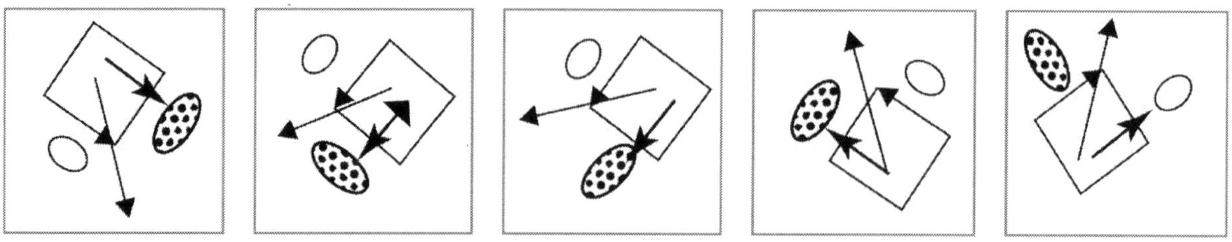

a b c d e

10.

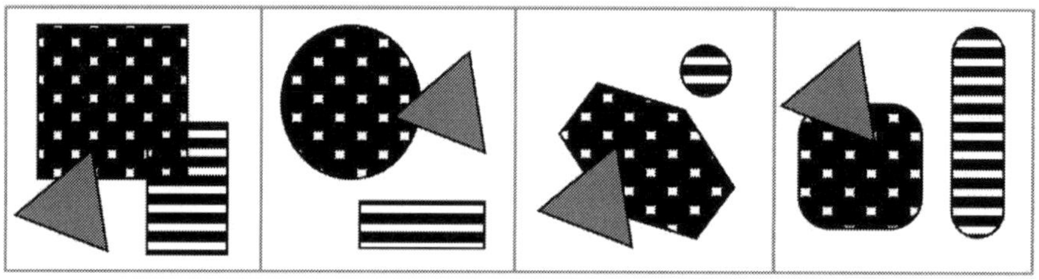

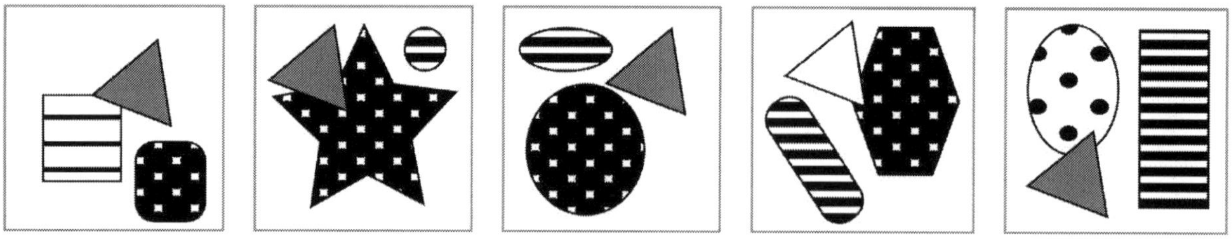

a b c d e

11.

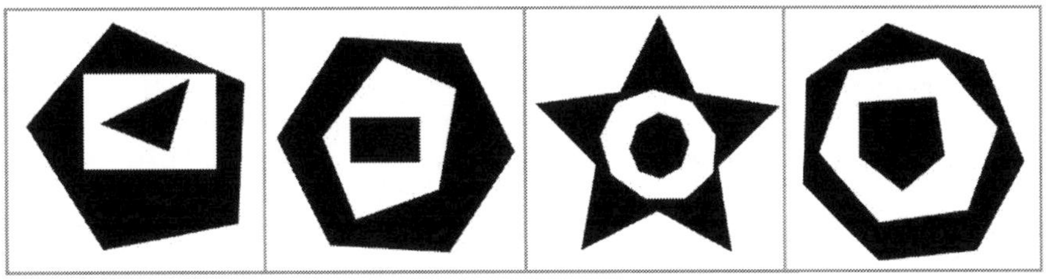

a b c d e

12.

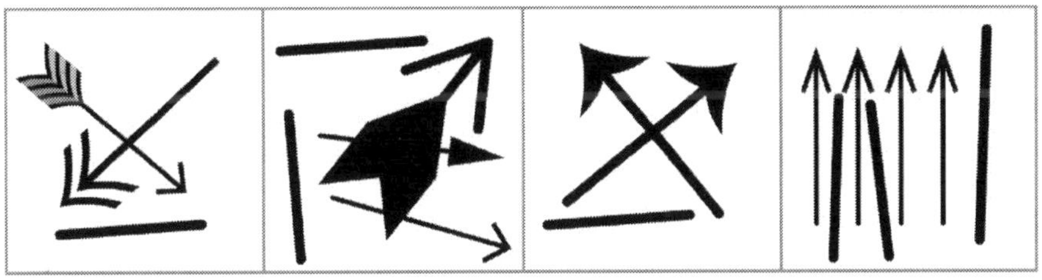

a b c d e

END OF SECTION 1 - PLEASE DO NOT TURN THE PAGE

Section 2 (Time allowed - 6 minutes)

For the next twelve questions, work out the code of the last picture and choose your answer from the five choices given.

Example:

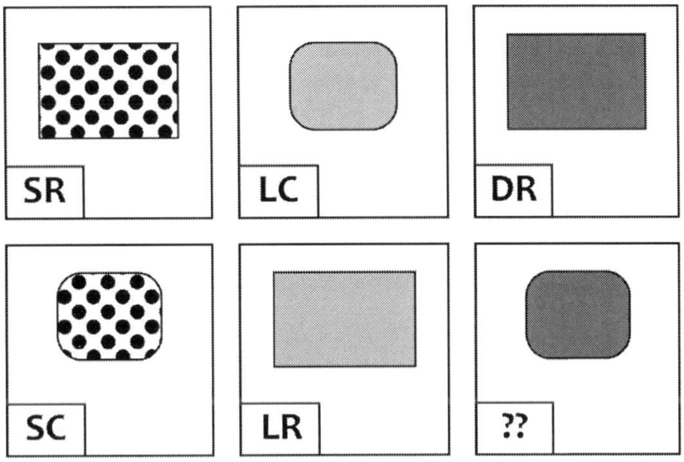

DC	DA	SR	SC	DL
(a)	b	c	d	e

The correct answer is: **a**

The code is: **D**=dark grey shading, **C**=rounded rectangle shape.

PLEASE WAIT UNTIL YOU ARE ASKED TO TURN OVER

13.

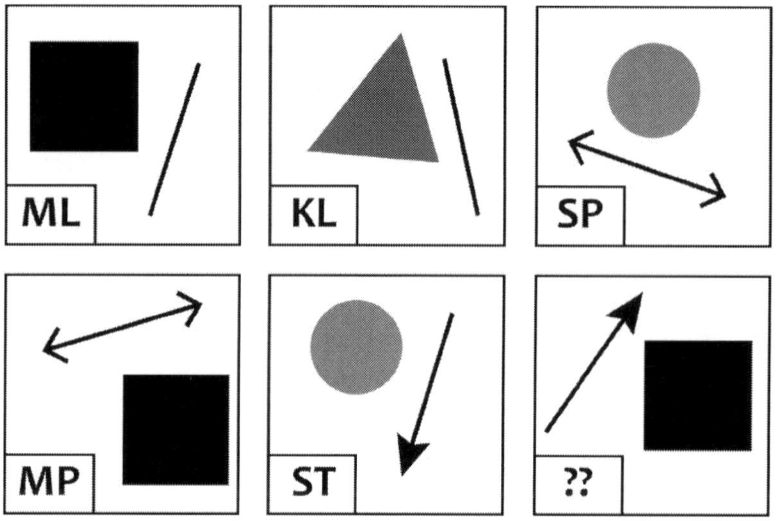

MT	KT	KP	MP	SL
a	b	c	d	e

14.

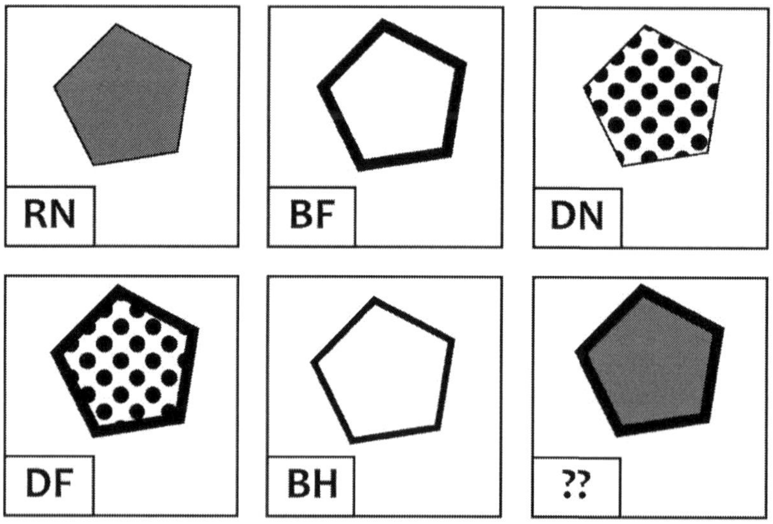

DF	BN	DH	RF	RH
a	b	c	d	e

15.

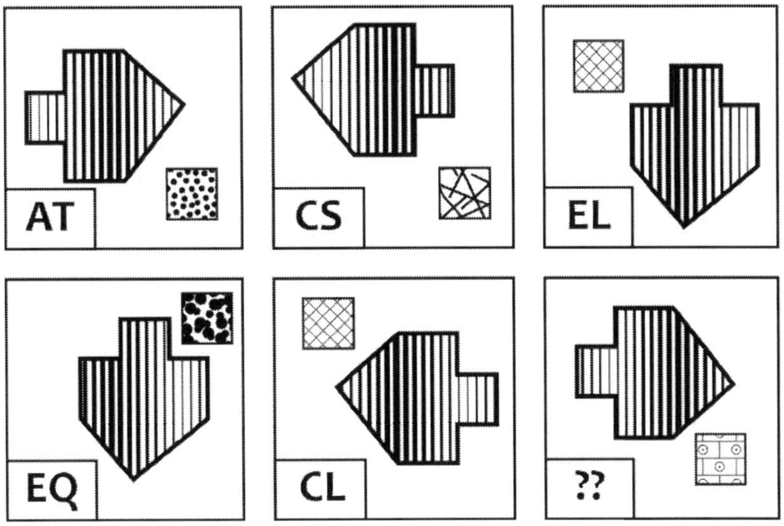

a	b	c	d	e
AQ	CK	AU	AS	QL

16.

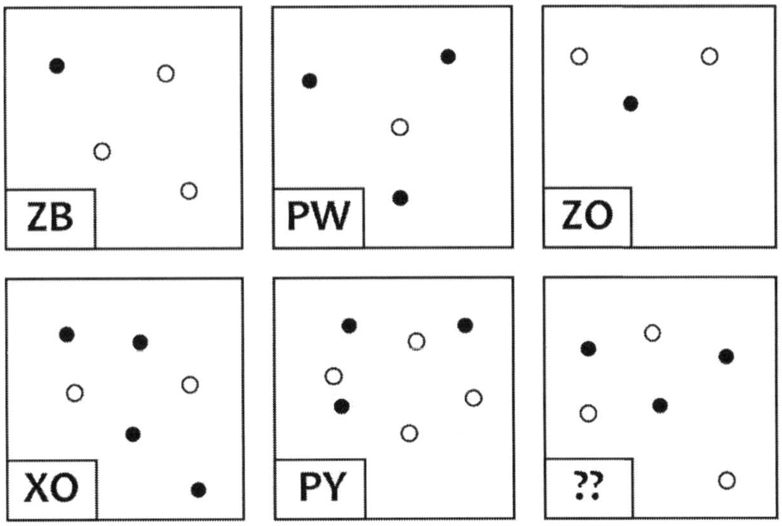

a	b	c	d	e
XB	ZB	ZN	PY	PB

PLEASE TURN THE PAGE AND CONTINUE

17.

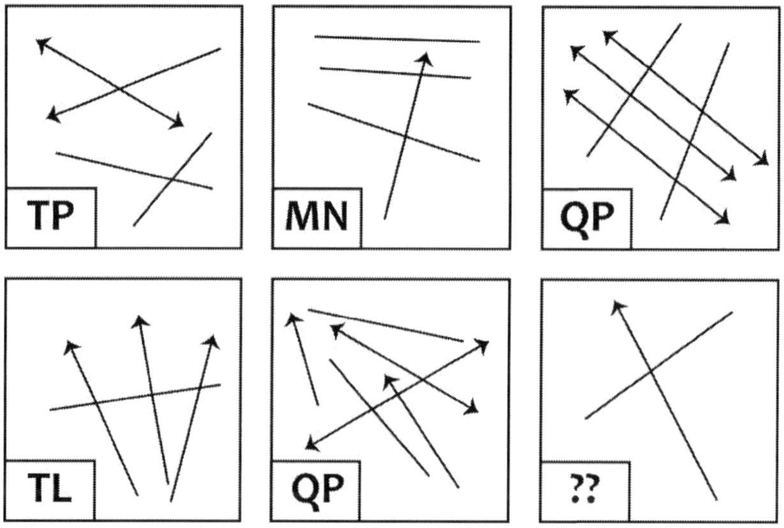

MQ	ML	TN	QL	MP
a	b	c	d	e

18.

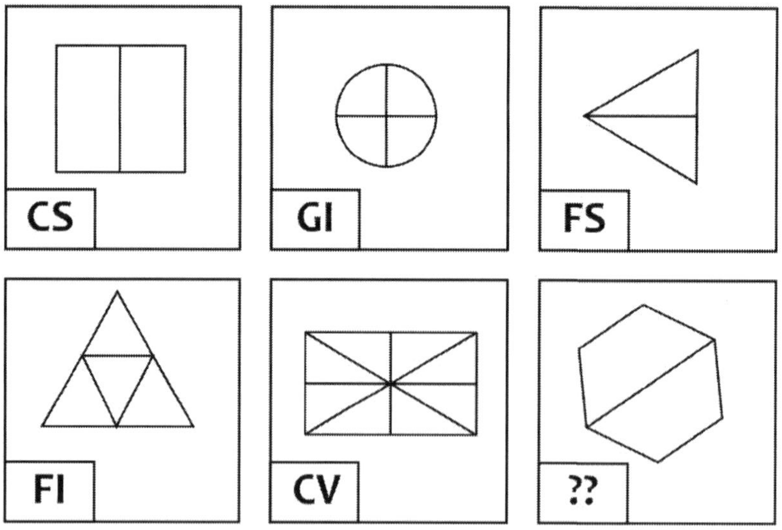

FV	GV	JV	CI	JS
a	b	c	d	e

19.

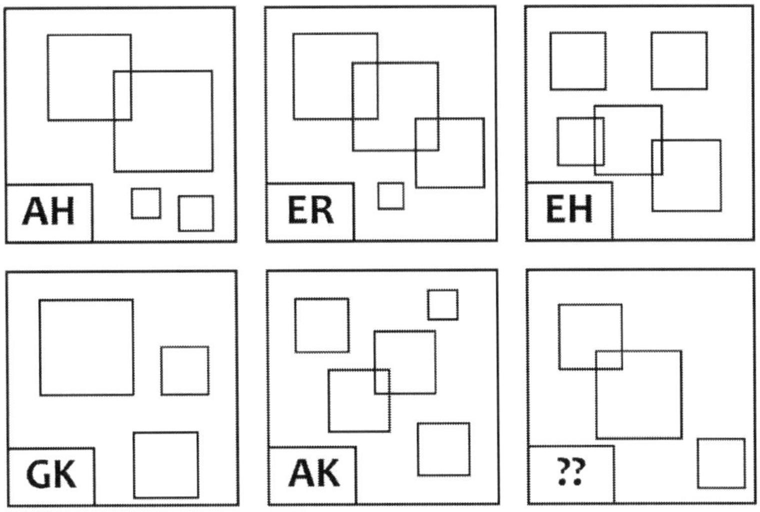

AR	EK	GH	AH	GR
a	b	c	d	e

20.

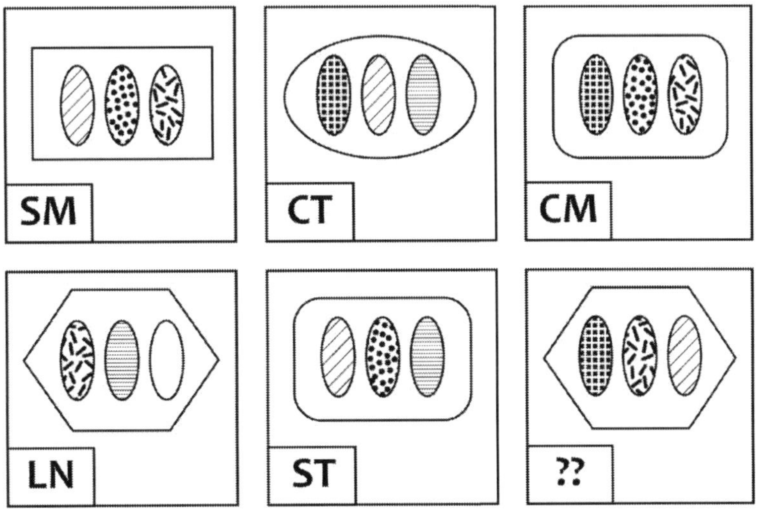

CD	CN	CM	SN	SD
a	b	c	d	e

PLEASE TURN THE PAGE AND CONTINUE

21.

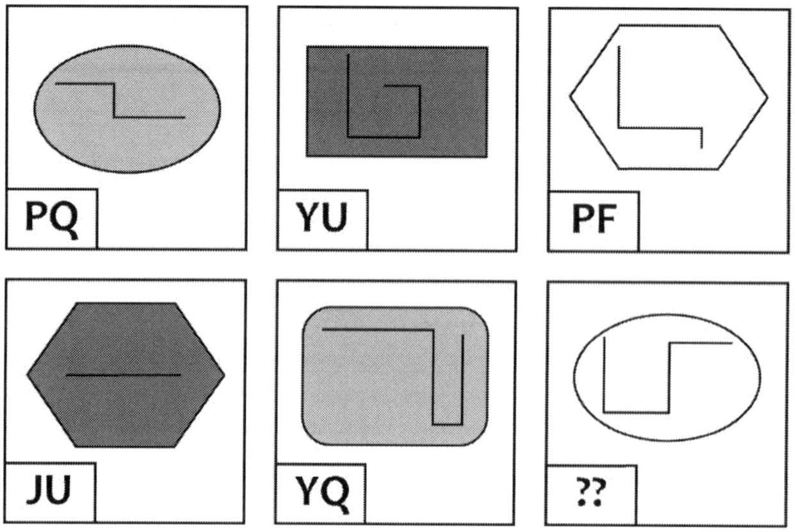

FY	YP	JF	YF	PU
a	b	c	d	e

22.

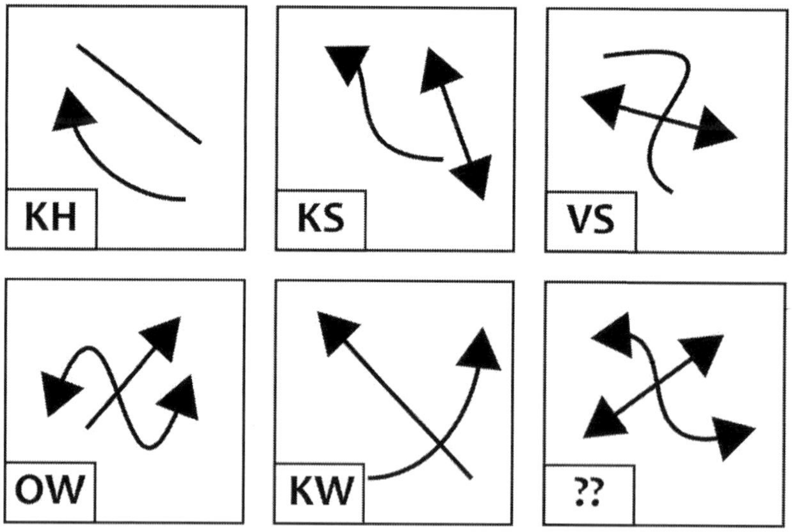

OS	VH	OH	VW	ON
a	b	c	d	e

23.

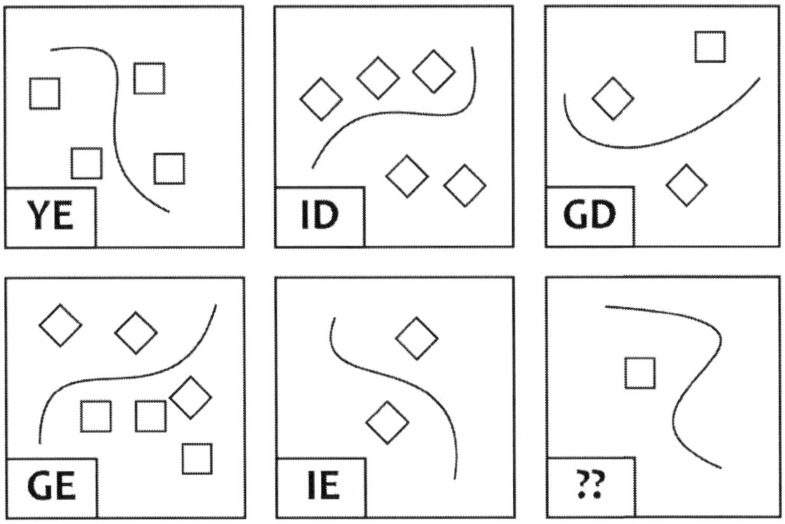

YE	IG	GR	YD	YJ
a	b	c	d	e

24.

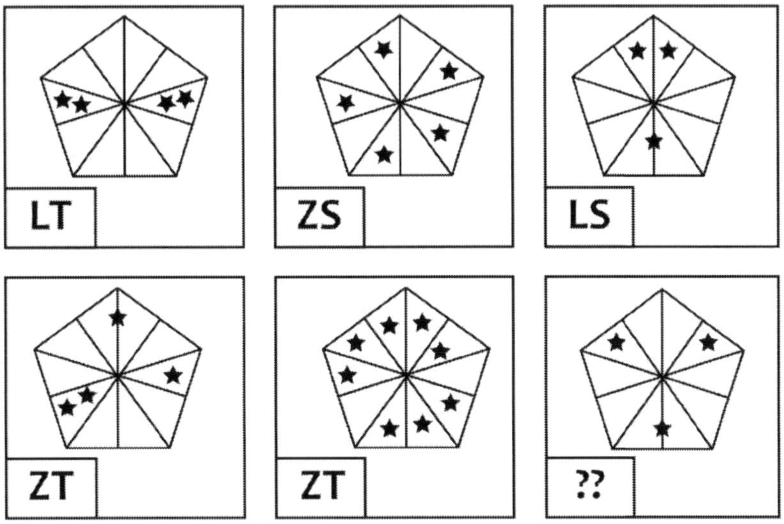

LS	LT	ZS	ZT	ZL
a	b	c	d	e

END OF SECTION 2 – PLEASE DO NOT TURN THE PAGE

Section 3 (Time allowed - 6 minutes)

For the next twelve questions, look at the 3D cube and then decide which net below it can be made to construct it. Only one net will work.

Example:

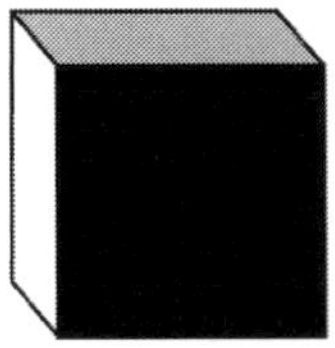

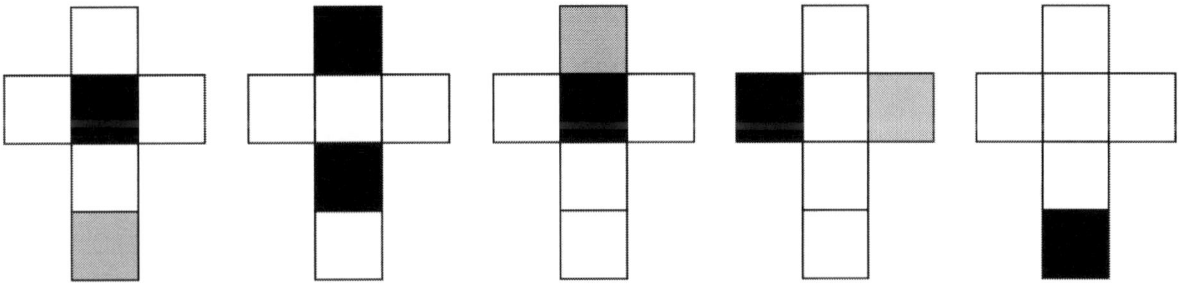

a b (c) d e

The correct answer is: **C**

This is the only net where a black face will touch a grey face.

PLEASE WAIT UNTIL YOU ARE ASKED TO TURN OVER

25.

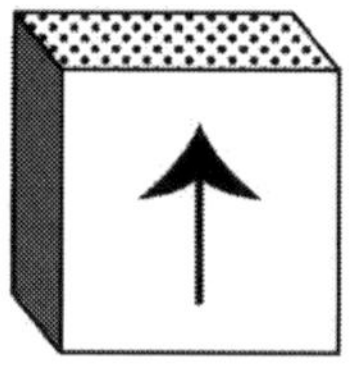

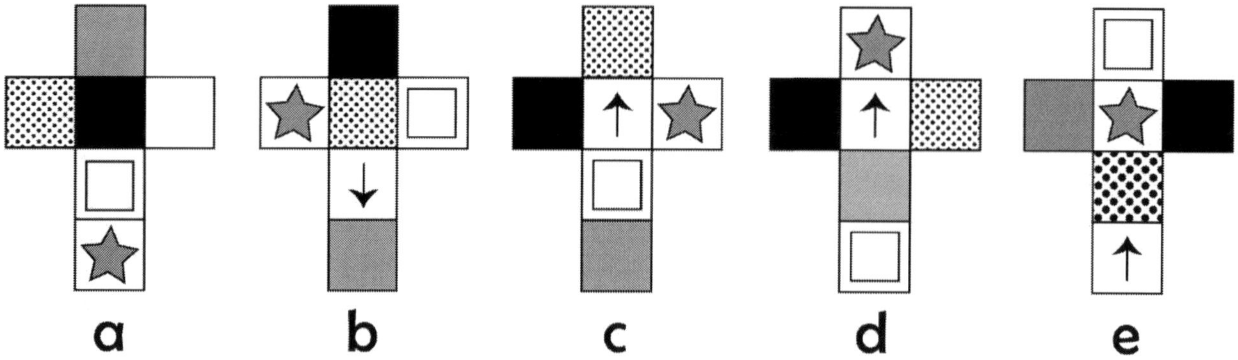

26.

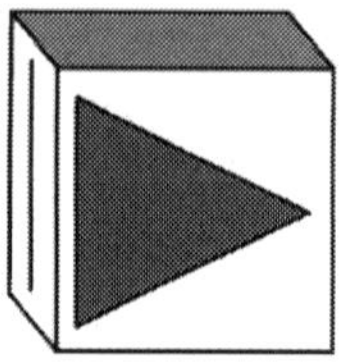

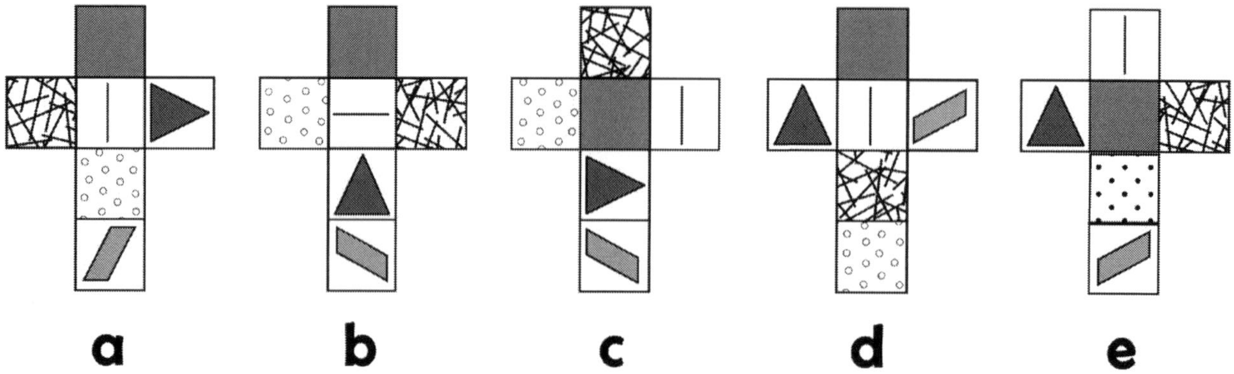

27.

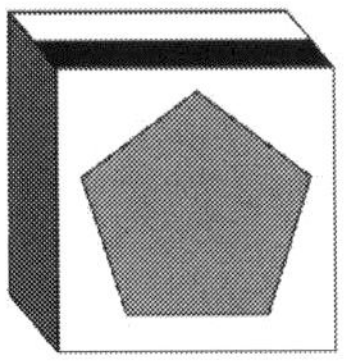

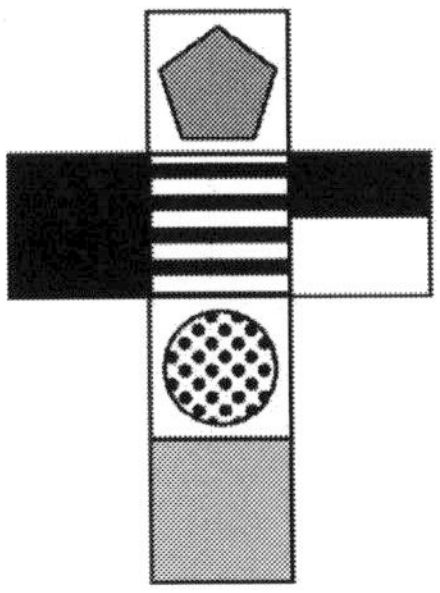

a

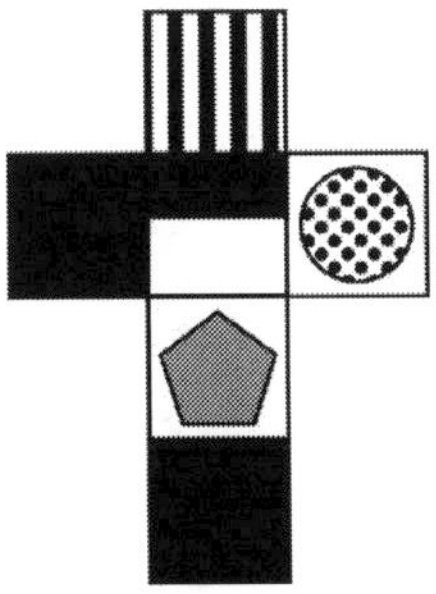

b

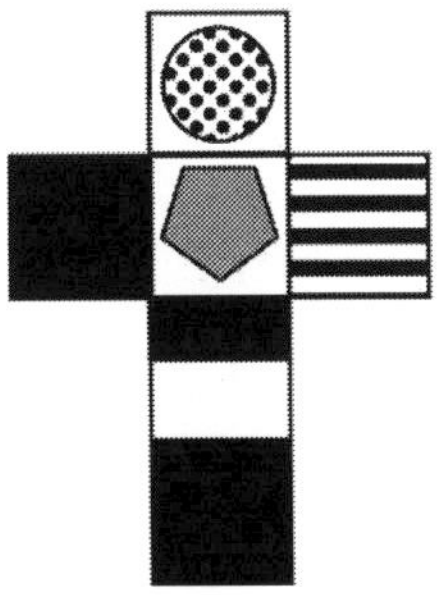

c

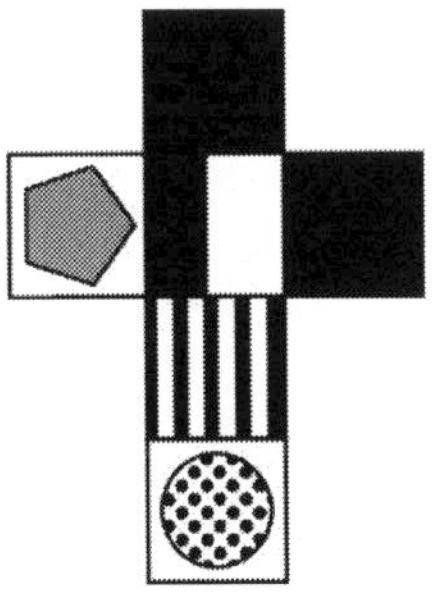

d

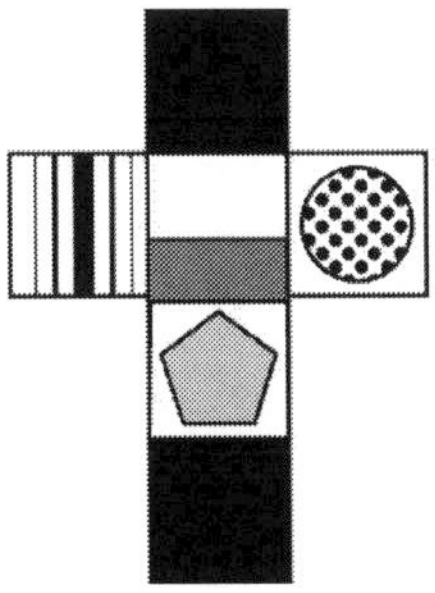

e

28.

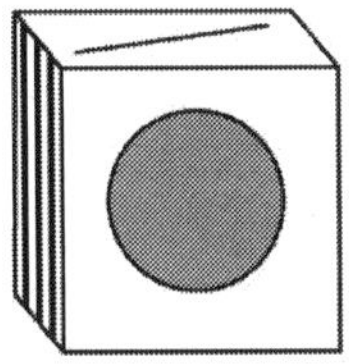

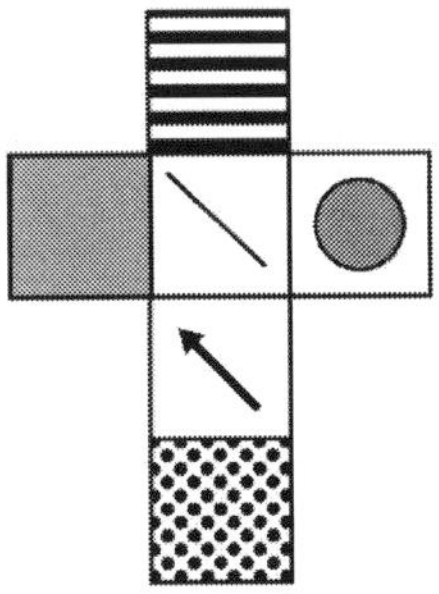

a

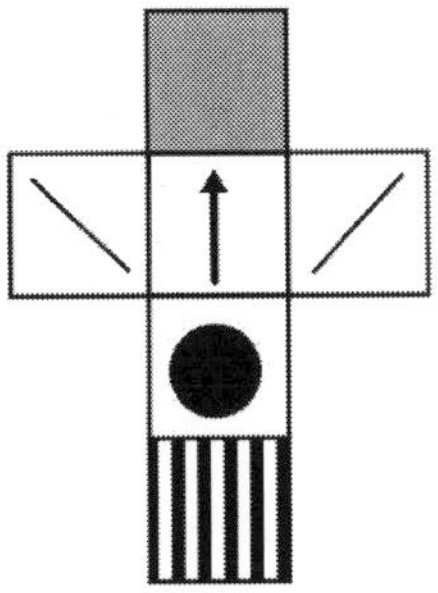

b

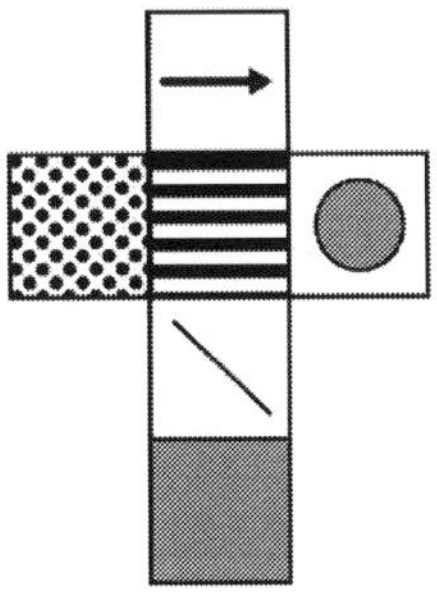

c

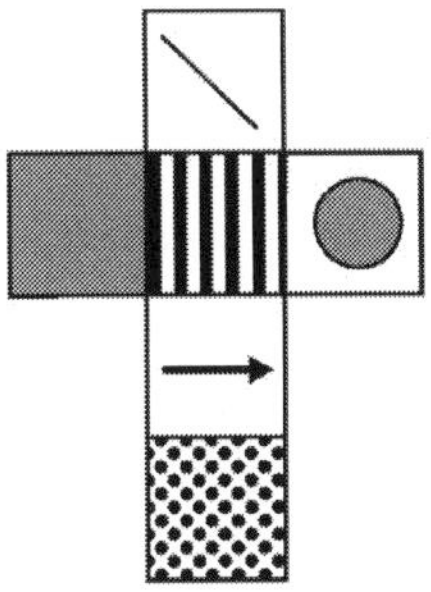

d

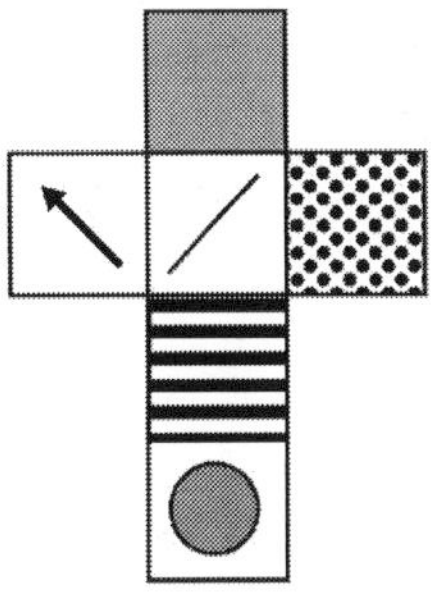

e

PLEASE TURN THE PAGE AND CONTINUE

29.

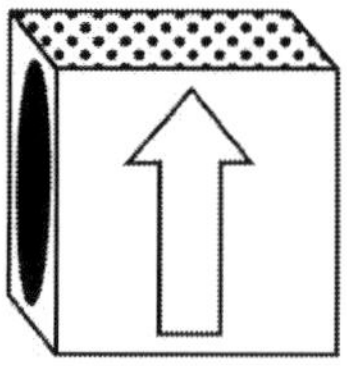

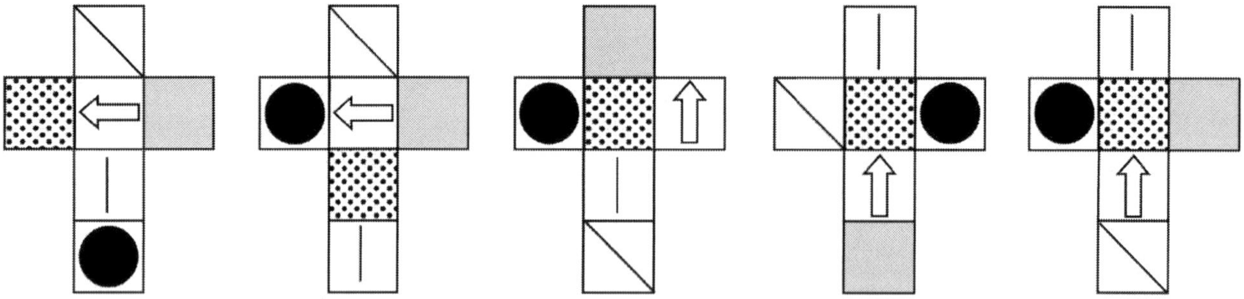

a b c d e

30.

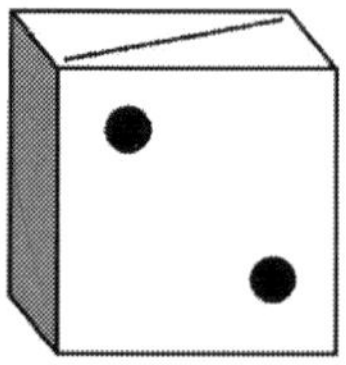

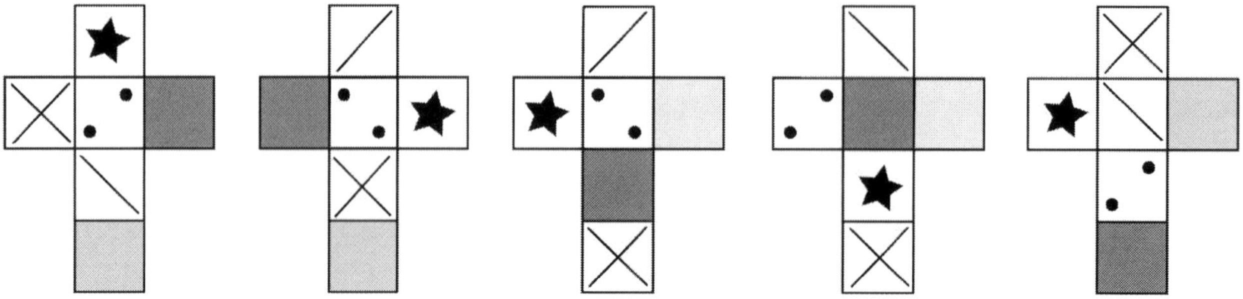

a b c d e

31.

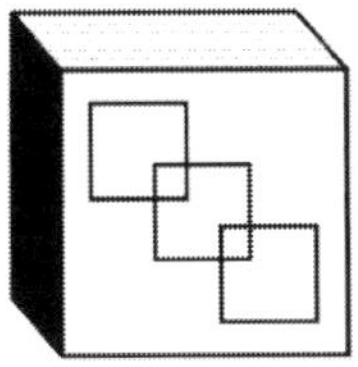

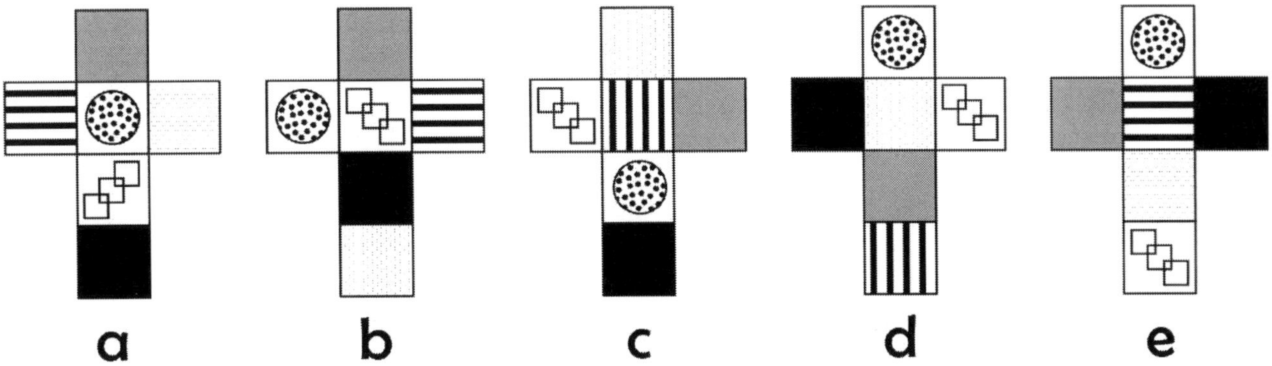

32.

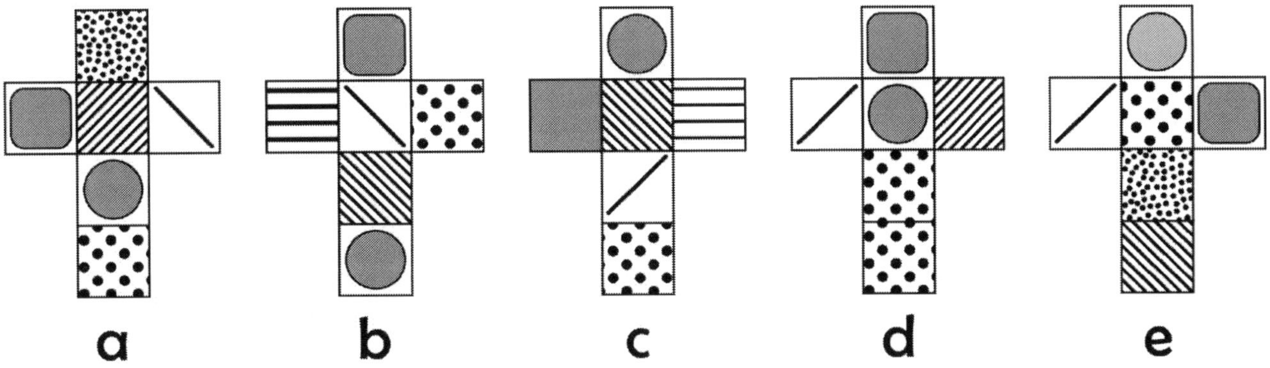

PLEASE TURN THE PAGE AND CONTINUE

33.

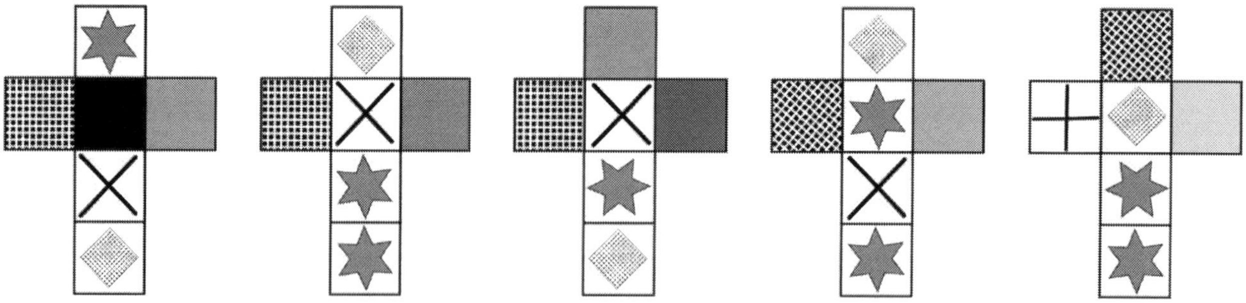

a b c d e

34.

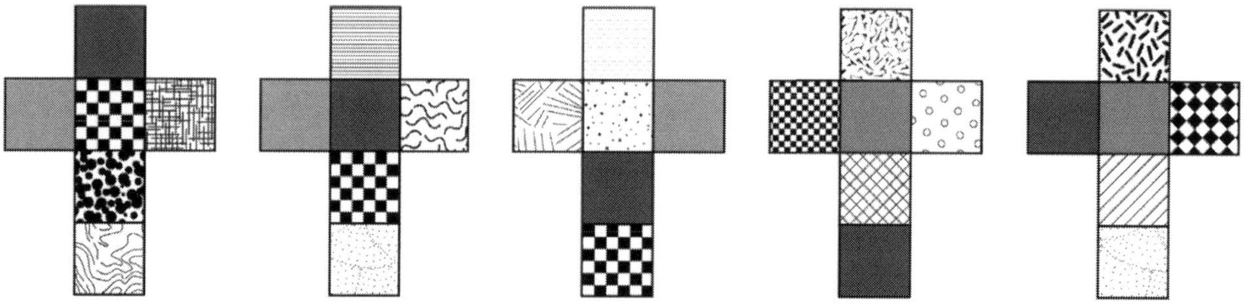

a b c d e

35.

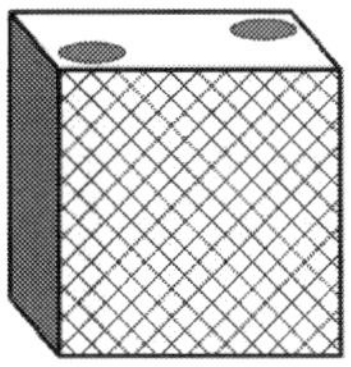

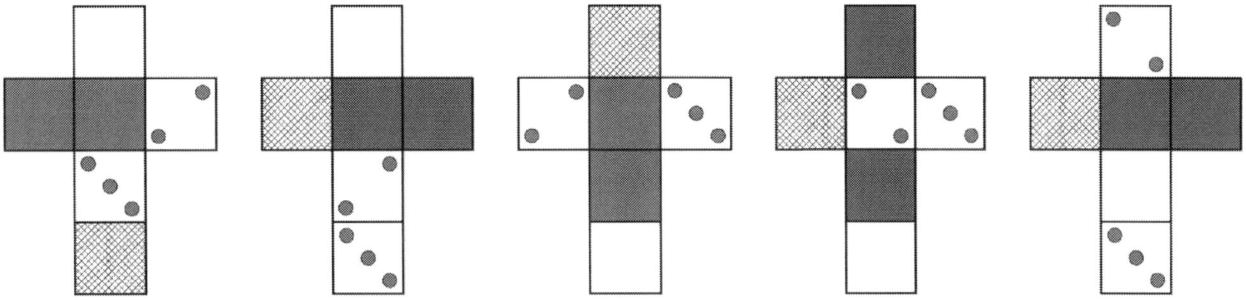

a b c d e

36.

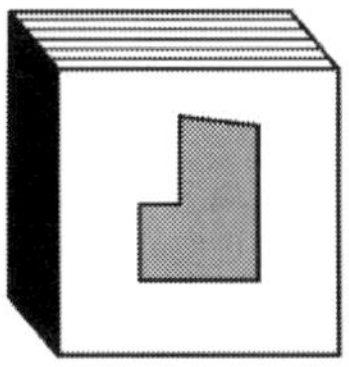

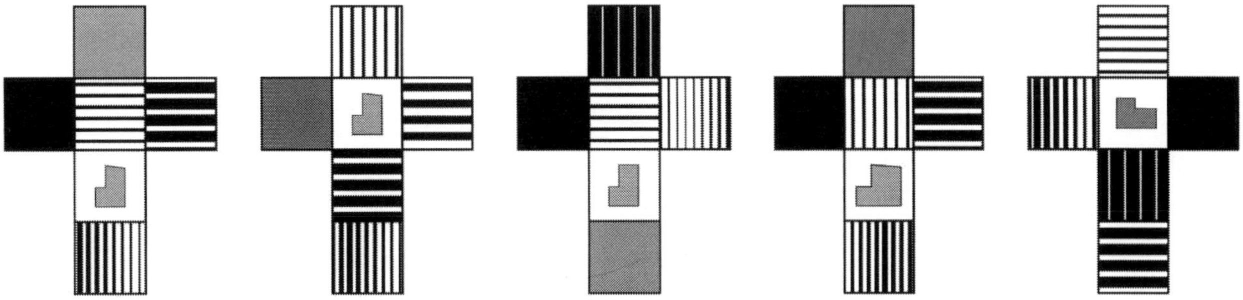

a b c d e

END OF SECTION 3 – PLEASE DO <u>NOT</u> TURN THE PAGE

Section 4 (Time allowed - 6 minutes)

Look at the grid and decide which of the five options would fit best in the space in the grid.

Example:

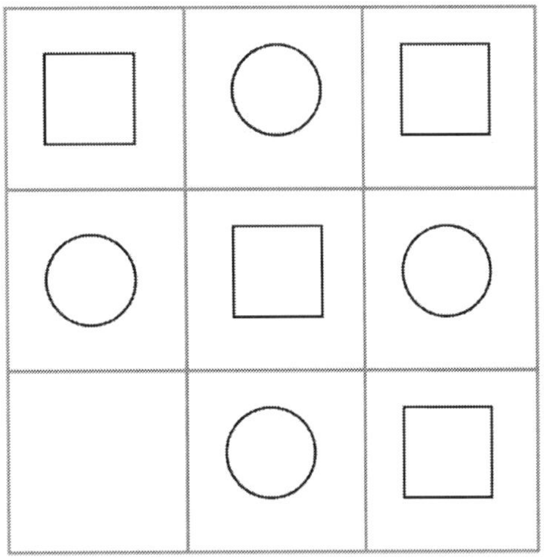

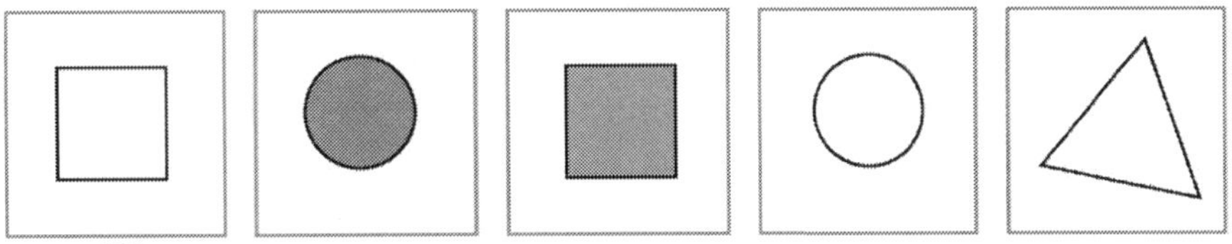

(a) b c d e

The correct answer is: a as the missing shape is a white square.

PLEASE WAIT UNTIL YOU ARE ASKED TO TURN OVER

37.

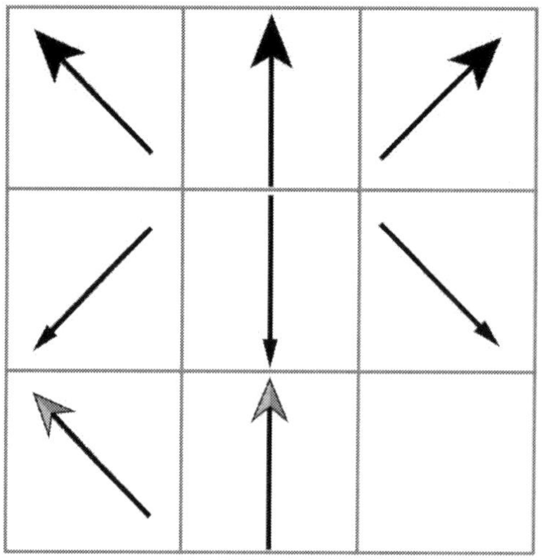

a b c d e

38.

a b c d e

39.

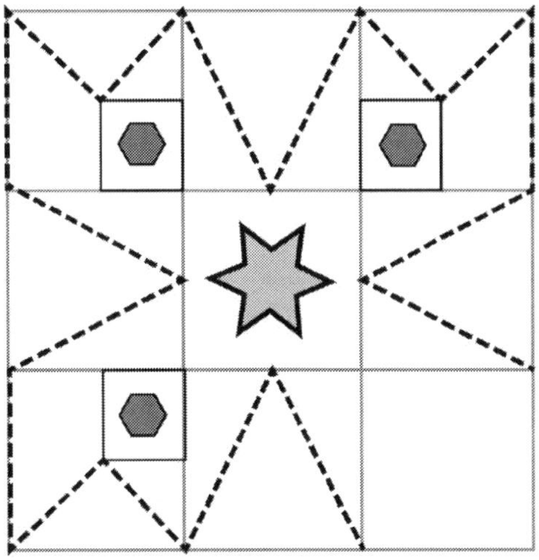

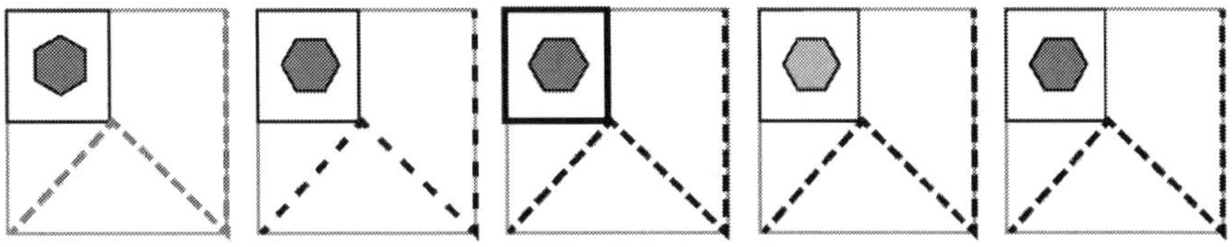

a b c d e

40.

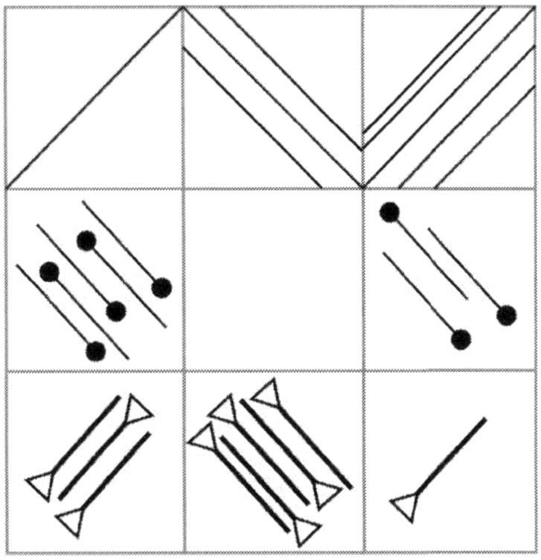

a b c d e

PLEASE TURN THE PAGE AND CONTINUE

41.

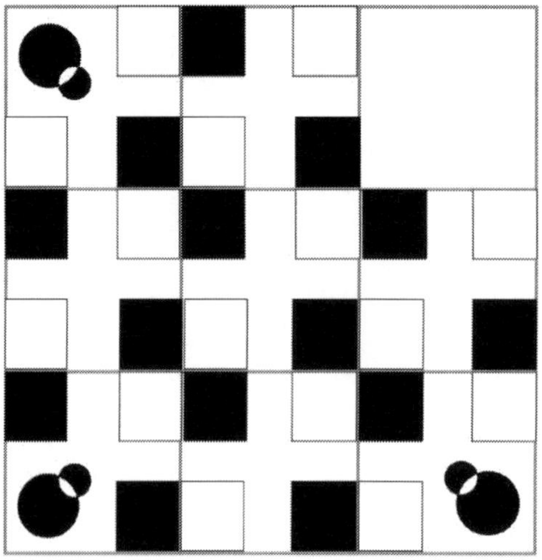

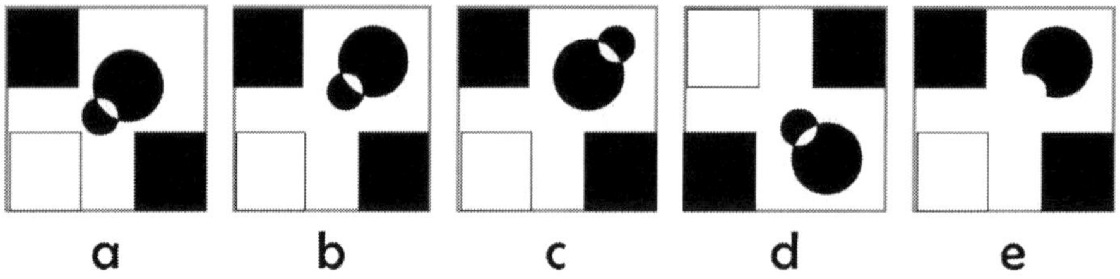

42.

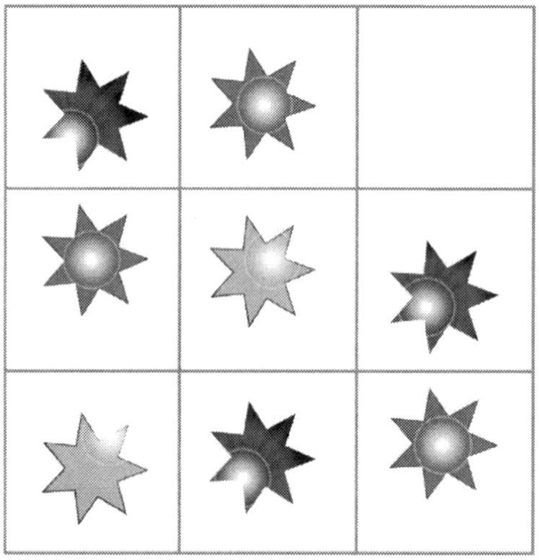

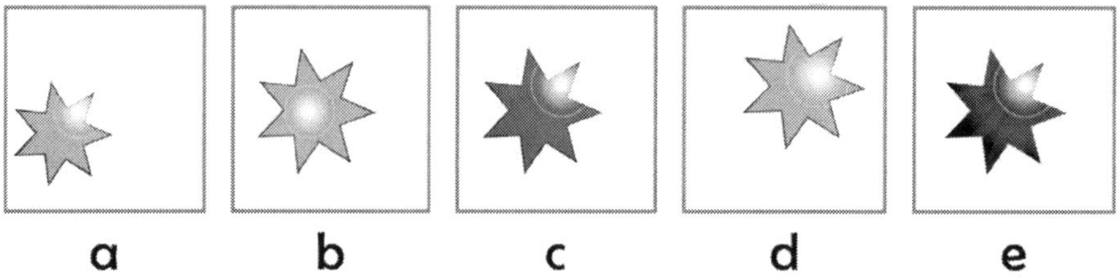

43.

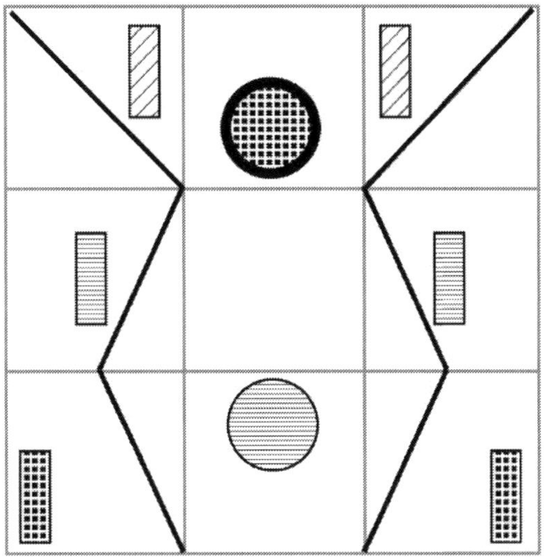

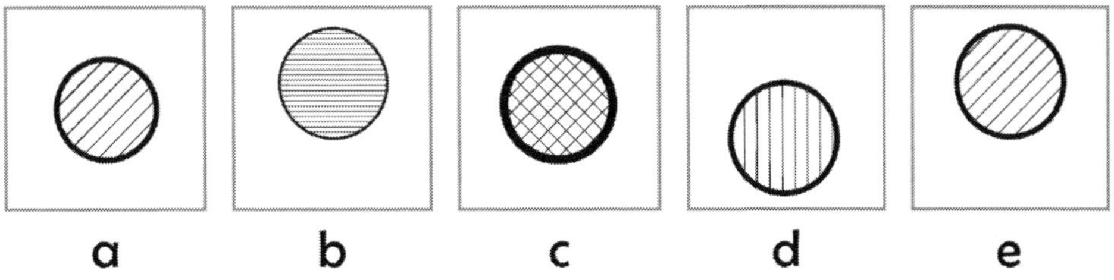

44.

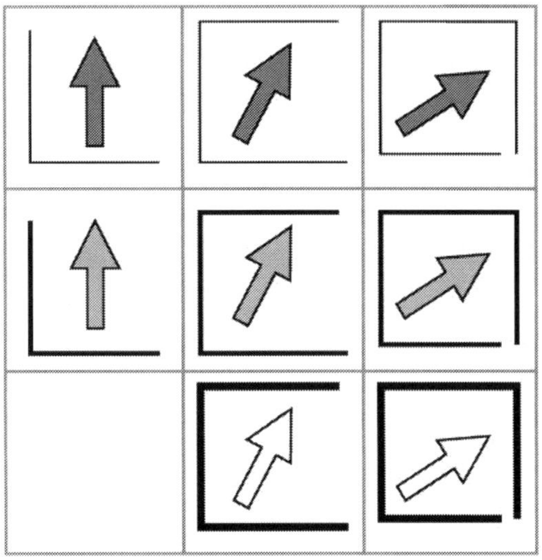

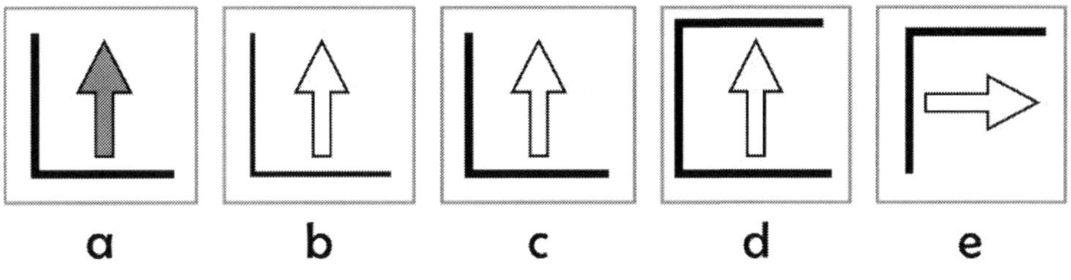

PLEASE TURN THE PAGE AND CONTINUE

45.

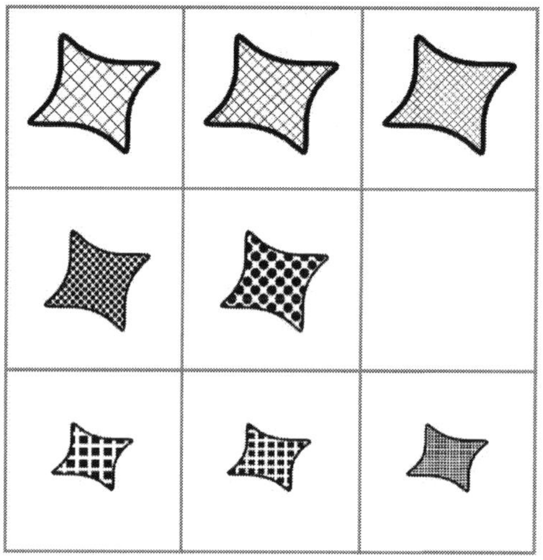

a b c d e

46.

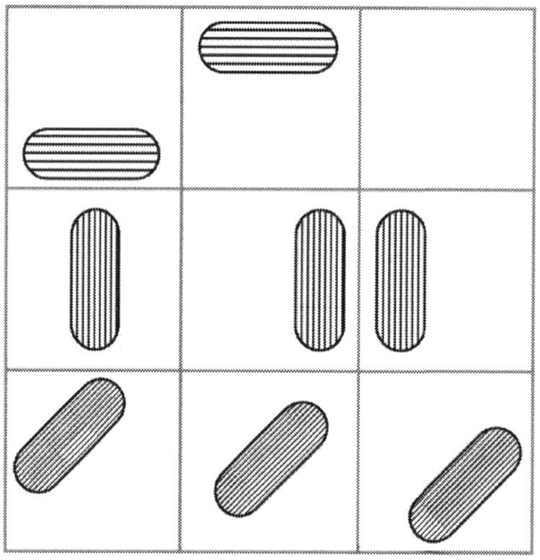

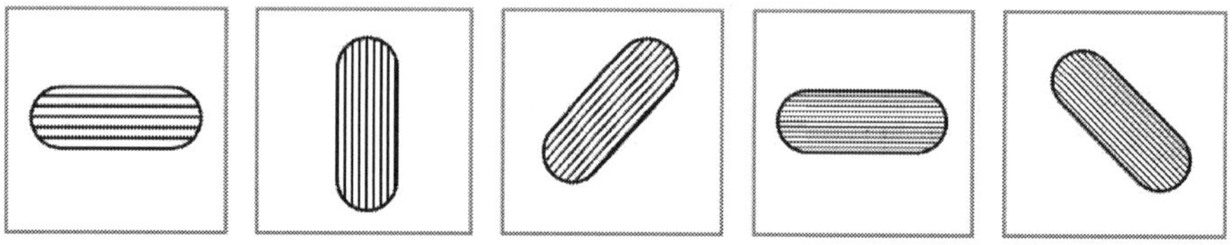

a b c d e

47.

a b c d e

48.

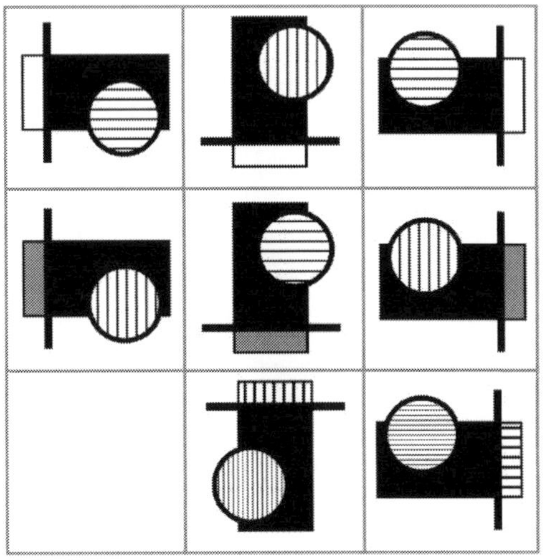

a b c d e

END OF SECTION 4 – TEST COMPLETE

WRITING

Paper 1

Instructions

1. You will have a writing task explained to you.

2. Once the task has been explained, you will be given time to plan and write.

3. You will have 40 minutes to complete your writing; this includes 10 minutes planning time.

WRITING TASK: Where in the world?

Either

(a) Describe in detail a recent holiday that you have been on to a different country from where you usually live. Explain who you went with and what you did.

or

(b) Write about a country that you haven't been to, but that you would really like to visit. Say why you want to go there and what you would do if you went.

Use the space below to plan your writing.
Option chosen: a or **b** (please circle your choice)

Write your composition on this page.

THE TEST IS COMPLETE – PLEASE ASK FOR EXTRA PAPER IF NECESSARY.

MATHS

Paper 2

Instructions

1. The questions are all multiple choice – choose only one answer for each question.

2. Answer as quickly and carefully as you can. If there is a question that you cannot do, leave it and go on to the next one.

3. After two practice questions, you have **25 minutes** to complete the test.

PRACTICE QUESTIONS (5 mins)

P1 What is 290 − 58.3?

A 231.3 **B** 229.8 **C** 231.7 **D** 230.5 **E** 229.1

P2. I buy a packet of biscuits for £1.90 which contains 10 biscuits. What is the cost per biscuit?

A £19 **B** 19p **C** £10 **D** 10p **E** £2.00

PLEASE WAIT UNTIL YOU ARE ASKED TO TURN OVER

1. The Venn diagram below shows which sports the children in Year 6 have played this week. How many children played tennis and rounders?

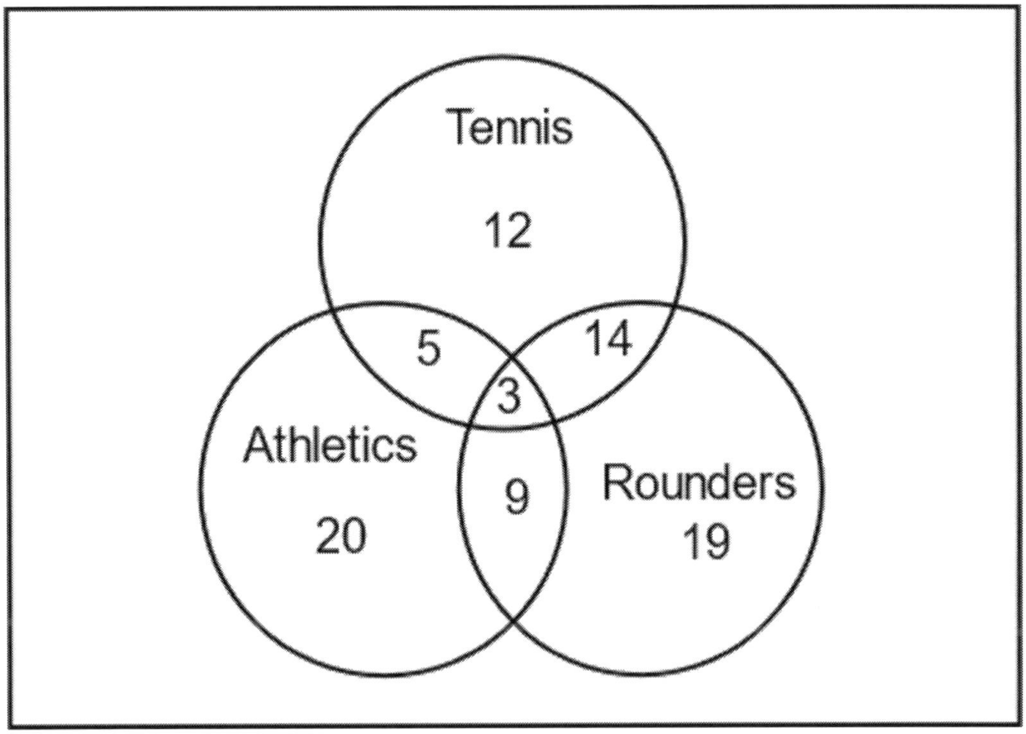

A 45 **B** 14 **C** 17 **D** 62 **E** 31

2. What is one quarter divided by one eighth?

A $\frac{1}{4}$ **B** $\frac{1}{2}$ **C** $\frac{1}{32}$ **D** 2 **E** 4

PLEASE TURN THE PAGE AND CONTINUE

3. Which of these shapes has the most lines of symmetry?

A rectangle **B** circle **C** regular pentagon

D cube **E** equilateral triangle

4. Felix was travelling from Sevenoaks to Sandwich, travelling at an average speed of 50mph. If the distance is 60 miles and he takes 1.5 hours to get there, stopping for a snack on the way, how long was his stop?

A 12 minutes **B** 18 minutes **C** 25 minutes

D 30 minutes **E** 45 minutes

5. What is the volume of this cylinder?
(Use a value of 3 for π)

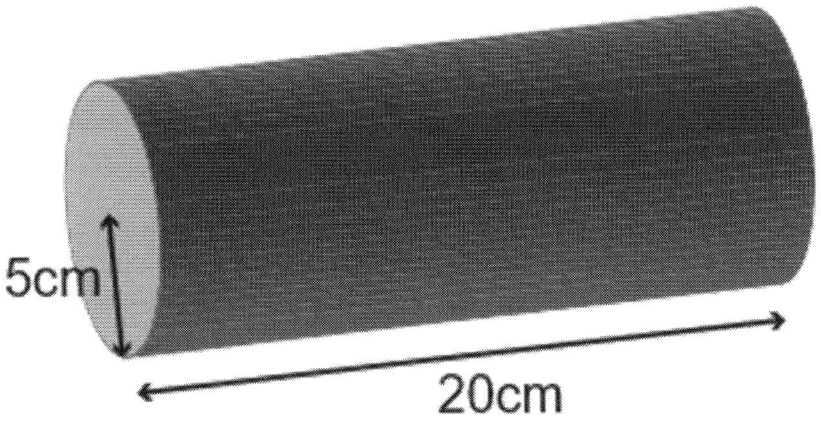

A $750cm^3$ **B** $1500cm^3$ **C** $150cm^3$ **D** $1500m^3$ **E** $100cm^3$

6. Which of the following words is symmetrical?

A **MILL** B **WEEDS** C **HOBBY**
D **HEED** E **MINIM**

PLEASE TURN THE PAGE AND CONTINUE

7. **What is** $12^2 - 16 \div 2 + \sqrt{9}$ **?**

A 139 **B** 67 **C** 73 **D** 141 **E** 1

8. **The angles in a quadrilateral are in the ratio 8:3:5:4 – what is the size of the largest angle?**

A 200° **B** 54° **C** 20° **D** 144° **E** 8°

9. **Each month Isobel, Ellie and Danny receive some money. Isobel receives 5 times as much as Ellie and Danny receives twice as much as Isobel. If they receive £320 in total, how much does Ellie get?**

A £10 **B** £20 **C** £30 **D** £40 **E** £50

10. **A train leaves the station at 13:49, travelling at 150km/hour. It travels for 375km before arriving at its destination. At what time does the train arrive?**

A 16:29 **B** 16:19 **C** 15:49 **D** 15:59 **E** 17:09

11. **Emily wins £200,000 in a competition. She gives 5% of her winnings to her sister and gives 10% to charity. How much does she have left?**

A £1000 **B** £20,000 **C** £30,000 **D** £140,000 **E** £170,000

12. **Look at the bar chart below. What is the mean average rainfall for the year?**

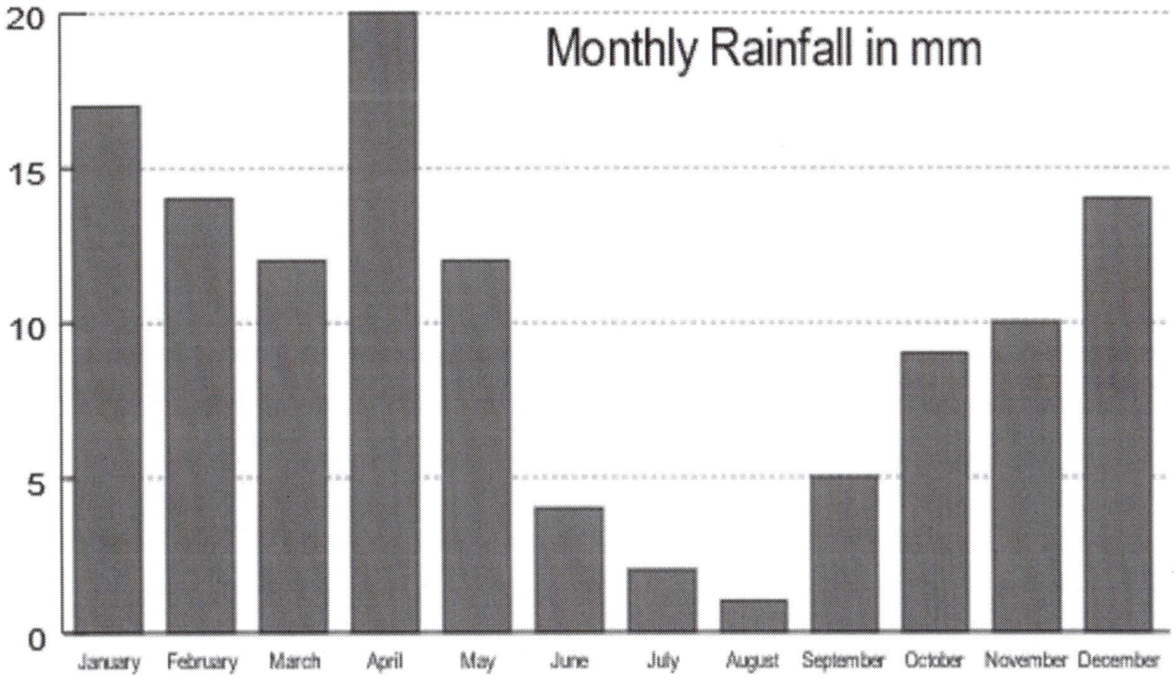

A 8mm **B** 10mm **C** 12mm **D** 15mm **E** 18mm

PLEASE TURN THE PAGE AND CONTINUE

13. The sum of three consecutive numbers is 171. What is the smallest number of the three?

A 55 **B** 56 **C** 57 **D** 58 **E** 59

14. Look at the diagram of Benny's garden. What is the area of the garden (shaded area) ?

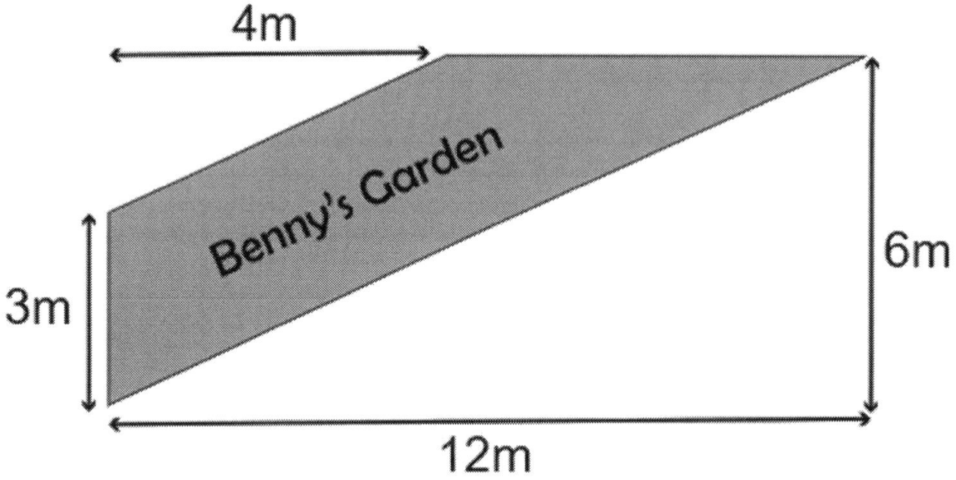

A $25m^2$ **B** $72m^2$ **C** $30m^2$ **D** $18m^2$ **E** $36m^2$

15. The mean mass of 7 dogs was 4.6kg. What was their total mass?

A 11.6 kg **B** 32.2 kg **C** 74.6 kg **D** 0.66 kg **E** 4.6 kg

16. **What is the ratio below expressed in its simplest form?**

150cm : 3km

A 150:3000 **B** 1500:3 **C** 1:2000 **D** 1:200 **E** 1:20

17. **Calculate the perimeter of the shape below, which has a vertical line of symmetry and a horizontal line of symmetry.**

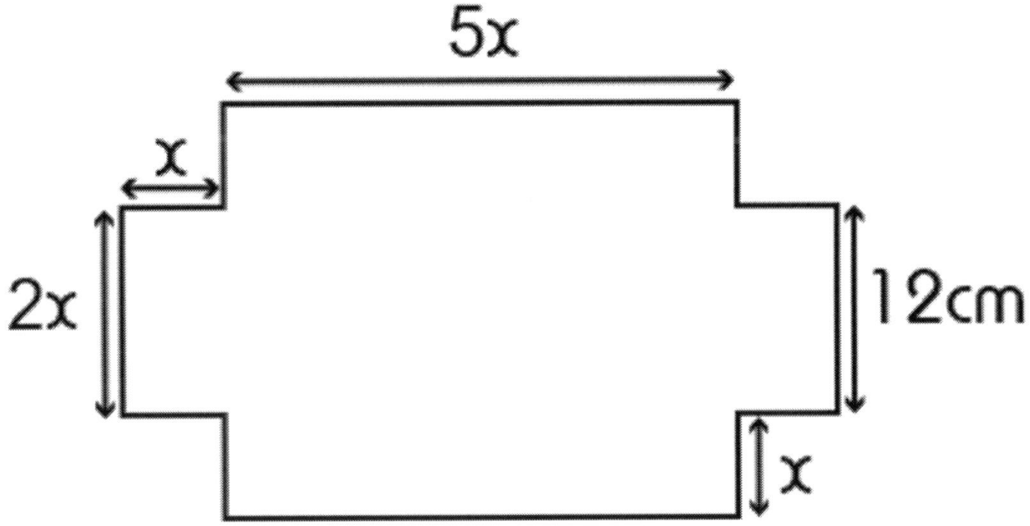

A 144cm **B** 162cm **C** 54cm **D** 60cm **E** 132cm

PLEASE TURN THE PAGE AND CONTINUE

18. **There are 9 red counters, 4 green counters, 10 blue counters and 13 yellow counters in a bag. What is the probability of picking out a counter that is *not* red?**

A 0.1 **B** 0.25 **C** 0.5 **D** 0.27 **E** 0.75

19. **What is** $\sqrt{6^2 + 4^3}$

A 100 **B** 10 **C** 24 **D** 1000 **E** 36

20. **Eleanor times herself running 100m in 15 seconds. What is her speed in km per hour?**

A 2.4 **B** 24 **C** 20.4 **D** 204 **E** 0.24

21. William cleaned cars to earn money for a holiday. He charged £4.50 per car. The table below shows how much money he made each day. How many cars did he clean over the whole week?

Sunday	Monday	Tuesday	Wednesday	Thursday	Friday	Saturday
£0	£18	£13.50	£40.50	£0	£13.50	£49.50

A 13 **B** 26 **C** 30 **D** 49 **E** 55

22. What is 20% less than 505?

A 101 **B** 404 **C** 606 **D** 909 **E** 485

23. What is 764.775 rounded to 2 decimal places?

A 765.75 **B** 765.77 **C** 764.77 **D** 764.78 **E** 764.776

PLEASE TURN THE PAGE AND CONTINUE

24. Chloe went shopping with £120.00 and spent £27.99 on a bag, £31.40 on some clothes and £4.50 on a milkshake. How much money did she have left?

A £36.11 **B** £104.39 **C** £15.61 **D** £56.11 **E** £63.89

25. *What is* $\frac{1}{3}$ *of* $\frac{1}{4}$ *of* 50% *of* 180**?**

A 90 **B** 7.5 **C** $\frac{1}{12}$ **D** $\frac{1}{24}$ **E** 4.167

THE MATHS SECTION OF THE TEST IS COMPLETE

PLEASE WAIT UNTIL YOU ARE ASKED TO TURN OVER

ENGLISH

Paper 2

Instructions

1. The questions are all multiple choice – choose only one answer for each question.

2. You have to read a passage and answer questions about it, as well as some additional questions about spelling, punctuation and grammar. You can look back at the passage as many times as you want.

3. Answer as quickly and carefully as you can. If there is a question that you cannot do, leave it and go on to the next one.

4. After two practice questions, you have **25 minutes** to complete the test.

PRACTICE QUESTIONS (5 mins)

P1. Which of these words is a verb?

A I **B** wear **C** a **D** big **E** hat

The correct answer is **B** wear; none of the other words are verbs

P2. How many of the words in the following sentence should have capital letters?

on tuesday I went to the shopping centre and on wednesday I went to london.

A four **B** five **C** six **D** seven **E** eight

The correct answer is **A** four:

On (beginning of sentence),
Tuesday,
Wednesday *and*
London (proper nouns)

PLEASE WAIT UNTIL YOU ARE ASKED TO TURN OVER

Read the following passage carefully and then answer the questions that follow:

Extract from "History Nuggets: Eleanor of Aquitaine"

In the Middle Ages, the wife of a French king became renowned in France and then later, also in England. She was reputed to be as beautiful as Cleopatra, as strong-willed as Queen Elizabeth I and as ready for battle as any warrior king. Yet, we don't know very much about her, compared to other prominent figures in history as very few contemporary documents exist. However, from what we do know, Eleanor of Aquitaine was one of the most influential women of the twelfth century and went on to have a pivotal role in English history.

On Good Friday, 1137, Eleanor's father died when she was aged thirteen. Her father, William, was count of Poitou and duke of Aquitaine. Eleanor, the oldest of his two daughters, became a highly sought-after bride as she would inherit her father's titles and land, including the vast region of Aquitaine which was the largest territorial principality in France.

The heir to the French Crown, King Louis the Younger, married her in July 1137 at the cathedral in Bordeaux and so when Louis became king of France less than a month later, Eleanor became queen. They ruled France together and Eleanor was very influential, making herself the chief advisor to her husband. However, their arranged marriage was not a happy one. Louis' character was the polar opposite of Eleanor's; he was subdued, pious and withdrawn whereas she was a woman of the world, erudite and energetic. Eventually they parted in 1152 when a French council declared their marriage to be illegal (in the Middle ages, divorce wasn't really possible).

Within a few weeks of the official annulment of her marriage to Louis, Eleanor was married again. She had been captivated by Henry Plantagenet, who was more youthful and energetic than Louis ever could be and also very educated. When Henry found out that Eleanor was available, a hasty wedding was arranged at Poitiers; it was arranged in secret and a simple ceremony unbecoming of the bride and groom's status.

Eleanor's second husband was duke of Normandy and had become count of Anjou after the death of his father in 1151. Combined with Eleanor's inheritance, they now ruled a substantial portion of France. Henry also inherited the title duke of Aquitaine and was now the largest of all French landowners (including the king) despite having no royal title.

Yet, the lack of royal title did not last for long as Henry was an heir to the English throne. When King Stephen died in 1154, nominating Henry as his successor, both Henry and Eleanor left France and travelled to England to be crowned. The first decade of their reign was harmonious, although Eleanor was left on her own for long periods whilst Henry was fighting abroad. She also bore Henry eight children: William, Henry, Matilda, Richard, Geoffrey, Eleanor, Joan and John. Five of these were male and could potentially continue the royal line.

Their first son, William, sadly died when he was a baby. Their second son, Henry – known as Young Henry – was crowned king when aged 15 but was too young to wield any power.

Richard became duke of Normandy and was crowned king in 1189, the same year that King Henry, Eleanor's husband, died. Known as 'Richard the Lionheart' because of his warrior reputation, he nevertheless needed Eleanor's help when he was held captive in Germany. She raised the ransom money and personally delivered it owing to her maternal devotion. Knowing Richard was safe, Eleanor retreated to France and withdrew from her royal duties.

Eleanor intended to live out the rest of her days at Fontevraud Abbey. She became more introspective and hoped to end her days there peacefully. When Richard died in 1199, he was buried there but Eleanor had to re-enter public life to campaign for her last son, John, to be king.

John, believed to have been his father's favourite son, did succeed Richard due to Eleanor's efforts. He is best remembered nowadays for his involvement with the Magna Carta peace treaty and for his role in reworkings of the Robin Hood legends.

Returning to the abbey again in 1200, Eleanor was tired and not a young woman anymore. Even so, she still could not retire in peace as John often needed her help. As she neared the end of her life, she realised that her empire would be unlikely to survive, but a more potent concern was her impending death and her immortal soul.

She found some comfort in her last days, until her death in 1204, as she oversaw the construction of a family mausoleum for her late husband, herself and Richard including life-size sculptures which still stand in the chapel at Fontevraud as a testament to Eleanor's dedication both to them and to her own legacy.

YOU MAY NOW TURN THE PAGE AND BEGIN ANSWERING THE QUESTIONS - YOU MAY REFER BACK TO THE PASSAGE AS MANY TIMES AS YOU WANT TO

1. What happened on Good Friday, 1137 that would change Eleanor's life dramatically?

A her father died
B she married a king
C she was very beautiful
D she was aged thirteen
E she became queen

2. Which word in the third paragraph (lines 12 – 19) means devout?

A subdued
B pious
C withdrawn
D erudite
E illegal

3. Which of these is closest in meaning to the word *captivated* as used on line 21?

A captured
B entranced
C pursued
D energised
E imprisoned

PLEASE TURN THE PAGE AND CONTINUE

4. Which two kings also had the title *duke of Normandy*?

A John and Richard
B Henry and John
C Henry and Richard
D William and Henry
E Young Henry and Richard

5. What did King Stephen do just before he died?

A went to France with Eleanor
B became heir to the throne
C told Eleanor that she would be queen
D told Richard that he despised him
E named Henry as his choice for king

6. Which of these words is the opposite of *harmonious* on line 32?

A tempestuous
B idyllic
C melodic
D discordant
E relentless

7. What does the following line mean (line 37)?

...he was too young to wield any power

A he was not old enough to be king
B he was too inexperienced to be powerful
C he was too immature to rule independently
D he was not strong enough to fight
E he had not yet learnt how to be a king

8. Which of these words does not adequately describe Eleanor's character as portrayed in the extract?

A dedicated
B forthright
C energetic
D inhibited
E knowledgeable

9. Why was the secret and unpretentious ceremony *unbecoming of the bride and groom's status* (line 24)?

A it was expected that royal weddings would be elaborate
B royal weddings were not allowed in the Middle Ages
C they couldn't afford a more regal ceremony
D the bride and groom were in hiding
E there weren't enough people to become guests

PLEASE TURN THE PAGE AND CONTINUE

10. Which of Henry and Eleanor's five sons is the youngest?

A William
B Young Henry
C Richard
D John
E Geoffrey

11. What does the phrase *maternal devotion* (line 42-43) imply about Eleanor?

A she was relentless in her desire for power
B she was not a good mother
C she was concerned about death
D she had a lot of children
E she cared deeply for her children

12. Which word in the paragraph from line 39-44 means *went back*?

A delivered
B raised
C ransomed
D withdrew
E retreated

The next five questions are about spelling. Read the sentence and locate the spelling error.

Circle the letter below the error or circle N if there isn't one.

13. King John was an enthusiastic hunter and rode a gray horse.
A B C D E N

14. He is portraid in a famous portrait pursuing a stag as his prey.
A B C D E N

15. He was also a connisseur of precious stones such as diamonds.
A B C D E N

16. John became notorious for his opulant and luxurious apparel.
A B C D E N

17. He was occasionally geniel but was frequently prone to rage.
A B C D E N

PLEASE TURN THE PAGE AND CONTINUE

The next five questions are about alphabetical order. For each question, choose the word that would be third if the words were in alphabetical order.

Example:

A banana **B** apple **C** lemon **D** melon **E** kumquat

The answer is E kumquat

18. **A** tired **B** tiered **C** tirade **D** triage **E** tepid

19. **A** corona **B** coronet **C** cornet **D** cornice **E** corroborate

20. **A** fraught **B** friend **C** frieze **D** fricassee **E** fraise

21. **A** envelop **B** environment **C** invade **D** invite **E** invincible

22. **A** tenuous **B** tempest **C** tenon **D** tent **E** temperature

For the next eight questions, choose the best word or phrase to fit in the gap.

23. Richard's claim to the throne was ___________ .

A deranged
B dubious
C derelict
D downright
E detail

24. Henry was ______________ to Eleanor of Aquitaine.

A relative
B cornered
C waiting
D ensnared
E betrothed

25. Young Henry was not interested in the day-to-day ___________ of the government.

A business
B character
C ministers
D future
E augmentation

PLEASE TURN THE PAGE AND CONTINUE

26. Joan was Eleanor's second youngest child; she was imprisoned ________ the new king of Sicily.

A for
B because
C by
D when
E if

27. In Medieval times, tournaments were very popular and ______ kings were expected to take part.

A expected
B strange
C such
D miriad
E even

28. ______________ King Stephen was unpopular, he built a powerful alliance with powerful barons.

A Although
B Despite
C Moreover
D Consequently
E Finally

29. Eleanor of Aquitaine was ________________ the richest queen in English history.

A preferably
B presently
C arguably
D antithesis
E remotely

30. There is a ____________ of historical documents pertaining to the period in which Eleanor lived.

A scant
B lack
C dirge
D lot
E excess

THE ENGLISH SECTION OF THE TEST IS COMPLETE

PLEASE DO NOT TURN THE PAGE

VERBAL REASONING

Paper 2

1. Read the instructions carefully for each set of questions.

2. You can continue until the end of the test.

3. You do not need to wait for further instructions once you have started.

DO <u>NOT</u> TURN THE PAGE UNTIL YOU ARE ASKED TO BEGIN

Section 1

Find two words, one from each group which are most <u>similar</u> in meaning. Circle both answers.

Example:

(great grate greet) (fire amazing hello)

(A) great	**X** fire
B grate	**(Y)** amazing
C greet	**Z** hello

The correct answers are **A** and **Y** as *great* can mean the same as *amazing*.

NOW TURN THE PAGE AND COMPLETE THE QUESTIONS IN THIS SECTION

1. (contemporary legion pulse) (antiquated legume heart)

A contemporary
B legion
C pulse

X antiquated
Y legume
Z heart

2. (relative descendent bacterial) (viral relationship virtual)

A relative
B descendent
C bacterial

X viral
Y relationship
Z virtual

3. (heavy lofty sparse) (metal hefty populated)

A heavy
B lofty
C sparse

X metal
Y hefty
Z populated

4. (resent repent forgive) (narrate exonerate reoffend)

A resent
B repent
C forgive

X narrate
Y exonerate
Z reoffend

5. (deny detain derail) (repudiate confess retract)

A deny	**X** repudiate
B detain	**Y** confess
C derail	**Z** retract

6. (articulate arrival ardent) (incoherent keen deflated)

A articulate	**X** incoherent
B arrival	**Y** keen
C ardent	**Z** deflated

7. (losing winsome forgetting) (victor fetching getting)

A losing	**X** victor
B winsome	**Y** fetching
C forgetting	**Z** getting

NOW CONTINUE WITH SECTION 2
YOU DO NOT NEED TO WAIT FOR FURTHER INSTRUCTIONS

PLEASE TURN THE PAGE AND CONTINUE

Section 2

In this section, work out the relationship between the first pair of words and then select the option that will complete the second pair in the same way.

Example:

Monday is to **Tuesday** as **Friday** is to...

A Saturday
B Sunday
C Wednesday
D Thursday
E Friday

The correct answer is **A** Saturday.

Monday relates to Tuesday as it is the next day of the week.
The correct day to follow Friday is Saturday.

NOW COMPLETE THE QUESTIONS IN THIS SECTION

8. Ice is to solid as milk is to...

A cow **B** gas **C** liquid **D** dairy **E** shake

9. Biscuit is to chef as wall is to...

A garden **B** builder **C** house **D** landscape **E** fall

10. Parliament is to owls as school is to...

A dogs **B** London **C** teachers **D** fish **E** children

11. Concerning is to about as returning is to...

A resuming **B** spinning **C** staying **D** crisis **E** chronic

PLEASE TURN THE PAGE AND CONTINUE

12. Impart is to convey as lead is to...

A head **B** teacher **C** procession **D** puppy **E** follow

13. Manuscript is to resign as walk is to...

A revise **B** travel **C** retake **D** paper **E** sprint

14. Technical is to expert as political is to...

A researcher **B** representative **C** current

D amateur **E** concurrent

15. Lease is to holder as van is to...

A road **B** trailer **C** navigation **D** guard **E** disappear

16. Rain is to control as sun is to...

A remote **B** lounge **C** equinox **D** replenish **E** descendant

PLEASE CONTINUE TO QUESTION 17

17. Read the following information, then find the correct answer from the options below.

Ken decides to have a race against four of his friends. Ronnie is the clear winner of the race. Emma finishes two places behind Tina, and Brian is the only competitor to fall over and not finish the race at all.

Who comes third in the race?

A Ken
B Ronnie
C Emma
D Tina
E Brian

NOW CONTINUE WITH SECTION 3
YOU DO NOT NEED TO WAIT FOR FURTHER INSTRUCTIONS

PLEASE TURN THE PAGE AND CONTINUE

Section 3

In each question, work out the missing number indicated by the question mark and select the correct answer from the options given.

Example:

4 8 12 [?] 20 24

A 10 **B** 11 **C** 16 **D** 13 **E** 14

The correct answer is **C** 16 as the numbers are going up in fours.

NOW COMPLETE THE QUESTIONS IN THIS SECTION

18. 18 36 72 [?] 288

A 411 **B** 144 **C** 141 **D** 108 **E** 136

19. [?] 58 51 45 40 36

A 68 **B** 64 **C** 69 **D** 66 **E** 62

20. 275 [?] 425 500 575

A 205 **B** 350 **C** 325 **D** 375 **E** 475

21. 9 9 18 27 45 72 [?]

A 117 **B** 108 **C** 126 **D** 153 **E** 180

PLEASE TURN THE PAGE AND CONTINUE

22. **1 8 27 [?] 125 216**

A 36 **B** 49 **C** 64 **D** 81 **E** 100

23. **1000 100 10 [?] 0.1**

A 110 **B** 1 **C** 0.01 **D** 101 **E** 10,000

24. **[?] 15 60 300 1800**

A 5 **B** 8 **C** 10 **D** 12 **E** 14

25. **52 264 476 688 [?]**

A 879 **B** 799 **C** 888 **D** 890 **E** 900

26. [?] 23 33 42 50

A 14 **B** 13 **C** 12 **D** 15 **E** 16

27. 998 877 655 [?]

A 402 **B** 302 **C** 332 **D** 344 **E** 322

NOW CONTINUE WITH SECTION 4
YOU DO NOT NEED TO WAIT FOR FURTHER INSTRUCTIONS

PLEASE TURN THE PAGE AND CONTINUE

Section 4

Use the alphabet to help you find the letter sequence that completes each sentence.

A B C D E F G H I J K L M N O P Q R S T U V W X Y Z

Example:

AB is to **CD** as **LM** is to...

A NO　　**B** NP　　**C** OP　　**D** PQ　　**E** PP

The correct answer is **A** NO

The first and second letters (A and B) each translate forward by two letters

A -> C and B-> D giving AB -> CD

Likewise, L and M will translate forward by one letter.

L -> N and M -> O giving LM -> NO so **A** NO is the correct choice.

NOW COMPLETE THE QUESTIONS IN THIS SECTION

A B C D E F G H I J K L M N O P Q R S T U V W X Y Z

28. **BZ** is to **CY** as **JR** is to...

A KQ **B** IS **C** MS **D** KT **E** KM

29. **Cf** is to **Ge** as **Ru** is to...

A St **B** vW **C** Uv **D** Vt **E** fC

30. **ACE** is to **GIK** as **CEG** is to...

A ILN **B** IKM **C** HJL **D** IJK **E** PRT

31. **MN** is to **KLOP** as **RS** is to...

A TUPQ **B** QRST **C** OQSU **D** OPST **E** PQTU

32. **BB** is to **wxy** as **GG** is to...

A bcd **B** dbc **C** bca **D** aBd **E** dCB

PLEASE TURN THE PAGE AND CONTINUE

A B C D E F G H I J K L M N O P Q R S T U V W X Y Z

33. **fH** is to **Ie** as **pQ** is to...

A RO **B** Ro **C** oR **D** or **E** Or

34. **JkM** is to **QrT** as **WxZ** is to...

A AbD **B** CeF **C** BcE **D** YzB **E** DeG

35. **TA** is to **Kr** as **CJ** is to...

A Wk **B** Mp **C** KR **D** Ta **E** Su

36. **cDjM** is to **AfHo** as **LvNn** is to...

A jXlP **B** JlxP **C** MjpX **D** DiKq **E** lJPi

NOW CONTINUE WITH SECTION 5

YOU DO NOT NEED TO WAIT FOR FURTHER INSTRUCTIONS

Section 5

In this section, first match the number codes to the letters.

One code is missing and will help you to answer the questions that follow.

Example:

H E L P **H Y P E** **T Y P E** **P E E L**

5 9 3 1 **8 4 1 9** **1 9 9 3**

What is the code for H Y P E?

A 5 9 3 1 **B** 8 4 1 9 **C** 1 9 9 3 **(D)** 5 4 1 9 **E** 5 9 9 3

The correct answer is **D** 5 4 1 9

The code 1 9 9 3 must be P E E L, therefore E is 9 and P is 1;
The code 5 9 3 1 must be H E L P, therefore H is 5;
The code 8 4 1 9 must be T Y P E, therefore Y is 4;

The code for H Y P E must then be H (5) Y (4) P (1) E (9) -> 5 4 1 9

NOW COMPLETE THE QUESTIONS IN THIS SECTION

PLEASE TURN THE PAGE AND CONTINUE

Solve the following code to answer the questions on this page.

P A I N T A N G G A N G P I N T

7 4 8 7 3 4 9 8 1 4 8 7

37. What is the code for G N A T ?

A 7 4 8 2 **B** 7 8 4 1 **C** 4 8 1 3

D 7 8 1 4 **E** 4 1 8 3

38. Which word does the code 7 4 9 8 represent?

A G A I N **B** G R A N **C** T I N G

D G A N E **E** G I N N

39. What is the code for G I A N T ?

A 7 4 9 1 8 **B** 7 4 8 9 2 **C** 7 9 8 4 1

D 9 1 8 4 7 **E** 7 9 4 8 1

Solve the following code to answer the questions on this page.

C H E E S E   S E A R C H
R E A S O N   A R C H E S

9 2 4 3 5 6   5 6 2 2 9 2   4 3 5 6 2 9

40. What is the code for S N A R E S ?

A 3 4 9 5 6 2   **B** 9 7 4 3 2 9   **C** 5 8 2 9 2 5

D 4 8 1 2 9 4   **E** 9 4 3 2 7 9

41. Which word does the code 9 8 8 7 2 3 represent?

A N O O S E S   **B** S P O O N S   **C** S O O N E R

D S E E I N G   **E** P O N D E R

42. What is the code for C H A S E R S ?

A 5 4 6 9 2 3 9   **B** 9 3 9 6 2 1 6   **C** 5 6 4 9 2 3 5

D 5 4 8 3 2 3 6   **E** 5 6 4 9 2 3 9

PLEASE TURN THE PAGE AND CONTINUE WITH SECTION 6

Section 6

In these questions, decide which of the choices can be rearranged to make another word that goes with the first two words.

Example:

WASHER **FRIDGE**

A R I D E R
B P O P E S
C L I O N S
D G R E E N
E A C I D S

The correct answer is A R I D E R

The letters R I D E R can be rearranged to make the word D R I E R.
The word D R I E R goes with W A S H E R and F R I D G E as they are all household appliances.

NOW COMPLETE THE QUESTIONS IN THIS SECTION

43. **ORANGES** **GRAPES**

A L I V E R
B S P O O N
C S A T E D
D D O W R Y
E S E P I A

44. **DONKEY** **ZEBRA**

A P L A I N
B G L O A T
C R I M E S
D S H O R E
E F R E E D

45. **GROCER** **PILOT**

A B R E A K
B G R A P E
C R E S I T
D M I N C E
E F R A M E

PLEASE TURN THE PAGE AND CONTINUE

46. **LUNGS** **BRAIN**

A L E A N S
B G R O A N
C P R I M E
D H E A L S
E P I N T S

47. **KILOMETRES** **INCHES**

A S T E E R
B V E A L S
C S L I M E
D S I N E W
E L O O P S

48. **PRIZE** **CUP**

A R E S I D E
B S L E E P Y
C H O U S E S
D G R I E V E
E D R A W E R

49. WEPT SOBBED

A D I C E R
B R I C E R
C R E S I T
D I N E P T
E T E N T S

50. WOODLAND COPPICE

A S O F T E R
B L O A F E R
C T I M E R S
D H E Y D A Y
E K N I G H T

51. STRONGER TALLER

A S M I L E
B S P E E D
C T O N E D
D W I R E D
E L I V I D

PLEASE TURN THE PAGE AND CONTINUE WITH QUESTION 52

52. Read the following information, then find the correct answer from the options below.

Silver is a metal that is used to make jewellery. Ellie has an oak jewellery box which contains a necklace and two pairs of earrings.

If the above statements are **true**, which of the following statements must also be true?

A Ellie likes jewellery.
B Ellie owns something made out of silver.
C All jewellery boxes are made out of wood.
D Ellie has a wooden jewellery box.
E All jewellery is made out of silver.

NOW CONTINUE WITH SECTION 7
YOU DO NOT NEED TO WAIT FOR FURTHER INSTRUCTIONS

Section 7

The word in square brackets has been made by using some of the letters from the words that are on either side. Make a new word for the middle of the second group in the same way and select this word from the options.

Example:

(main [lime] teal)   (riot [?] snub)

A barn   **B** born   **C** bean   **D** bane   **E** ball

The correct answer is **B** born

The first letter of the middle word is the same as the last letter of the second;
The second letter of the middle is the same as the third letter of the first;
The third letter of the middle is the same as the first letter of the first word;
The fourth letter of the middle word is the same as the second letter of the second word;

In this example, this means that the first letter of the answer must be B, the second O, the third R and the fourth N.

NOW TURN THE PAGE AND COMPLETE THE QUESTIONS IN THIS SECTION

53. **(arid [part] type)** **(into [?] gush)**

A sing **B** song **C** ring **D** rang **E** hang

54. **(arts [rail] line)** **(apse [?] swat)**

A says **B** pays **C** pore **D** paws **E** tape

55. **(epee [tree] tart)** **(seas [?] trap)**

A peas **B** teas **C** ease **D** saps **E** pass

56. **(word [rend] wren)** **(have [?] skin)**

A wine **B** vine **C** kine **D** kite **E** vane

57. **(seem [ease] same)** **(need [?] song)**

A gone **B** gran **C** sand **D** dene **E** nose

58. (tire [riot] rode) (demo [?] flag)

A gold **B** golf **C** fold **D** meld **E** mold

59. (dark [cars] scam) (fear [?] this)

A heat **B** hand **C** fish **D** reef **E** hire

60. (frog [goal] call) (shop [?] user)

A pose **B** rose **C** rush **D** push **E** ruse

NOW CONTINUE WITH SECTION 8
YOU DO NOT NEED TO WAIT FOR FURTHER INSTRUCTIONS

PLEASE TURN THE PAGE AND CONTINUE

Section 8

In each group, three words go together and two are the odd ones out. Decide which two do not go with the other three.

Circle both answers.

Example:

A train **(B) window** **C bus** **(D) runway** **E aeroplane**

The correct answers are **B** window and **D** runway. The other three words are all modes of transport making *window* and *runway* the odd ones out.

NOW COMPLETE THE QUESTIONS IN THIS SECTION

61. **A** malicious
B unkind
C happy
D cruel
E content

62. **A** assist
B hamper
C hinder
D basket
E impede

63. **A** reside
B dwelling
C home
D inhabit
E live

64. **A** apiary
B apathy
C contentment
D influence
E influenza

PLEASE TURN THE PAGE AND CONTINUE

65. **A** accessory
B refuse
C royalty
D regalia
E accoutrement

66. **A** create
B demolish
C annihilate
D build
E raze

67. **A** earthquake
B upstream
C homely
D relinquish
E grasshopper

68. **A** port
B wine
C star
D liner
E anchor

NOW CONTINUE WITH SECTION 9

YOU DO NOT NEED TO WAIT FOR FURTHER INSTRUCTIONS

Section 9

Use the alphabet to solve these codes.

A B C D E F G H I J K L M N O P Q R S T U V W X Y Z

Example:

If the code for **PLACE** is **OKZBD**, which of these is the code for **HOUSE**?

A GNTRD **B AGHRS** **C MKIUY**

D POSWL **E OJOLL**

The correct answer is **A** GNTRD
Each letter in the word is changed to the letter that comes before it in the code:

NOW TURN THE PAGE AND COMPLETE THE QUESTIONS IN THIS SECTION

A B C D E F G H I J K L M N O P Q R S T U V W X Y Z

69. **If the code for** PEANUT **is** ODZMTS**, which of these is the code for** ORANGE?

A NQZOFD **B** NQZMFD **C** NQBMFD

D NQZNFD **E** NSZMFD

70. **If the code for** STARLIGHT **is** TVDVQONPC**, which of these is the code for** STARTLING?

A TVDVYSVP **B** TVDYRPVP **C** TVDQONCP

D TVDVYRPVP **E** TVDVYRVPV

71. **If the code for** CARTOON **is** ACOWKSI**, which of these is the code for** DONKEY?

A BQKNAC **B** BQKNCA **C** BQJNAC

D BQKMCA **E** BQKMAC

A B C D E F G H I J K L M N O P Q R S T U V W X Y Z

72. **If the code for** HEAVENLY **is** ICDRJHSR, **which of these words would produce the code** QJDJJ?

A PLAIN **B** PLANT **C** PLANE

D PRONE **E** PRICE

73. **If the code for** SUMMER **is** RWJQZX, **which of these words would produce the code** MKDLO?

A NIGHT **B** LIGHT **C** NINES

D NOTES **E** LATER

NOW CONTINUE WITH SECTION 10

YOU DO NOT NEED TO WAIT FOR FURTHER INSTRUCTIONS

PLEASE TURN THE PAGE AND CONTINUE

Section 10

Work out the missing numbers by working out how the number in the first set of square brackets has come from and then applying the same method to the second set of numbers.

Example:

3 [21] 7   4 [?] 2

A 2   **B** 4   **C** 6   **(D)** 8   **E** 10

The correct answer is **D**

In the first set of numbers, the 7 and 3 are multiplied to get 21.
In the second set of numbers, therefore, the solution is 4 x 2 = 8

NOW TURN THE PAGE AND COMPLETE THE QUESTIONS IN THIS SECTION

74. **5 [11] 55** **10 [?] 90**

A 10 **B** 9 **C** 12 **D** 5 **E** 3

75. **2 [25] 12** **6 [?] 7**

A 8 **B** 12 **C** 43 **D** 62 **E** 80

76. **17 [23] 20** **27 [?] 31**

A 30 **B** 21 **C** 44 **D** 35 **E** 16

77. **8 [32] 8** **7 [?] 10**

A 17 **B** 52 **C** 64 **D** 70 **E** 35

78. **18 [144] 90** **75 [?] 55**

A 99 **B** 40 **C** 130 **D** 10 **E** 72

79. **100 [5] 25** **200 [?] 20**

A 11 **B** 12 **C** 13 **D** 14 **E** 15

80. **2 [40] 100** **7 [?] 5**

A 6 **B** 7 **C** 8 **D** 9 **E** 10

THE VERBAL REASONING TEST IS COMPLETE

PLEASE DO NOT TURN THE PAGE

NON-VERBAL REASONING

Paper 2

Instructions

1. The questions are all multiple choice – choose only one answer for each question.

2. Answer as quickly and carefully as you can. If there is a question that you cannot do, leave it and go on to the next one.

3. You will be given instructions about each section and the amount of time you have to complete it.

Section 1 (Time allowed - 6 minutes)

For the next twelve questions, look at the figure with a dotted line where it will be folded. One of the five options below it shows what it will look like when folded (although it may be rotated). Select the correct one.

Example:

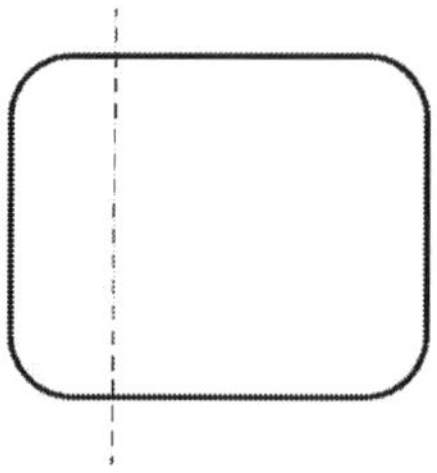

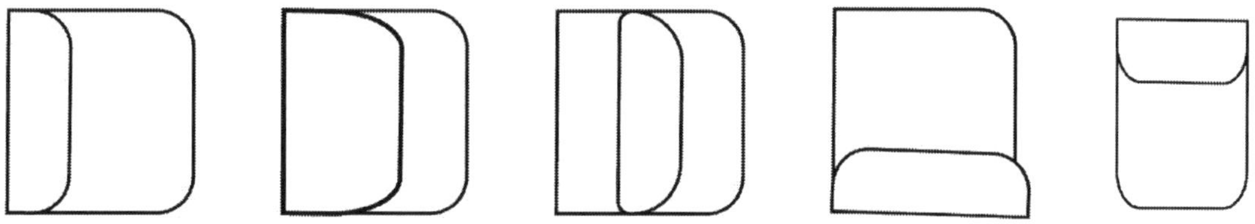

(a) b c d e

The correct answer is: a

PLEASE WAIT UNTIL YOU ARE ASKED TO TURN OVER

1.

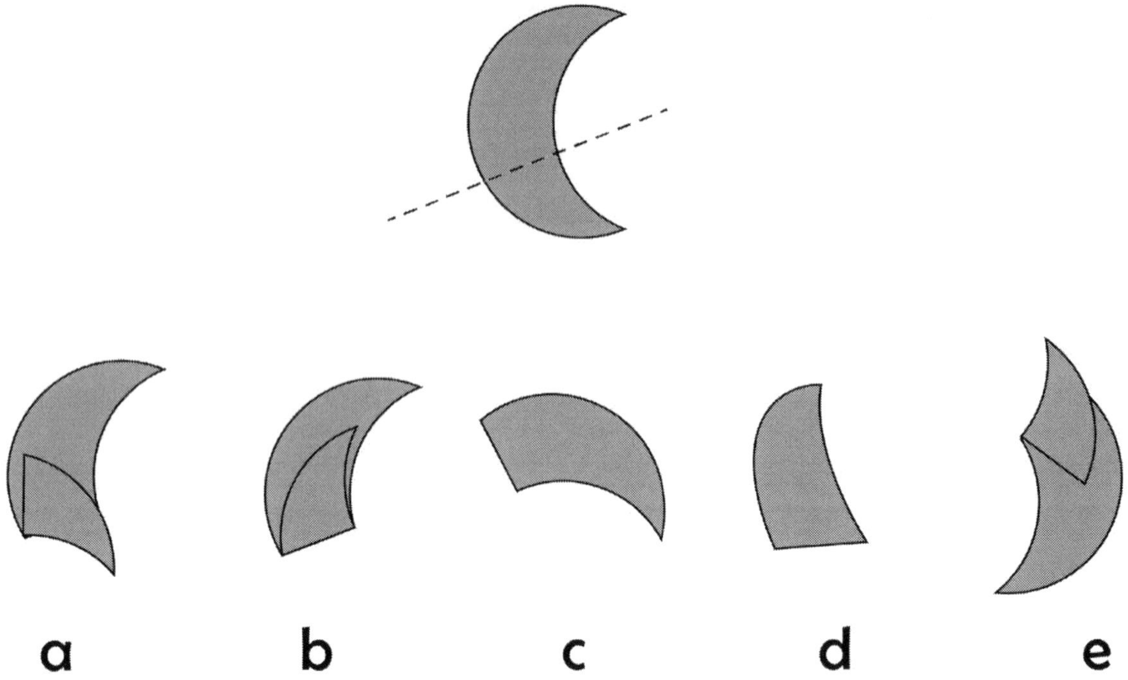

2.

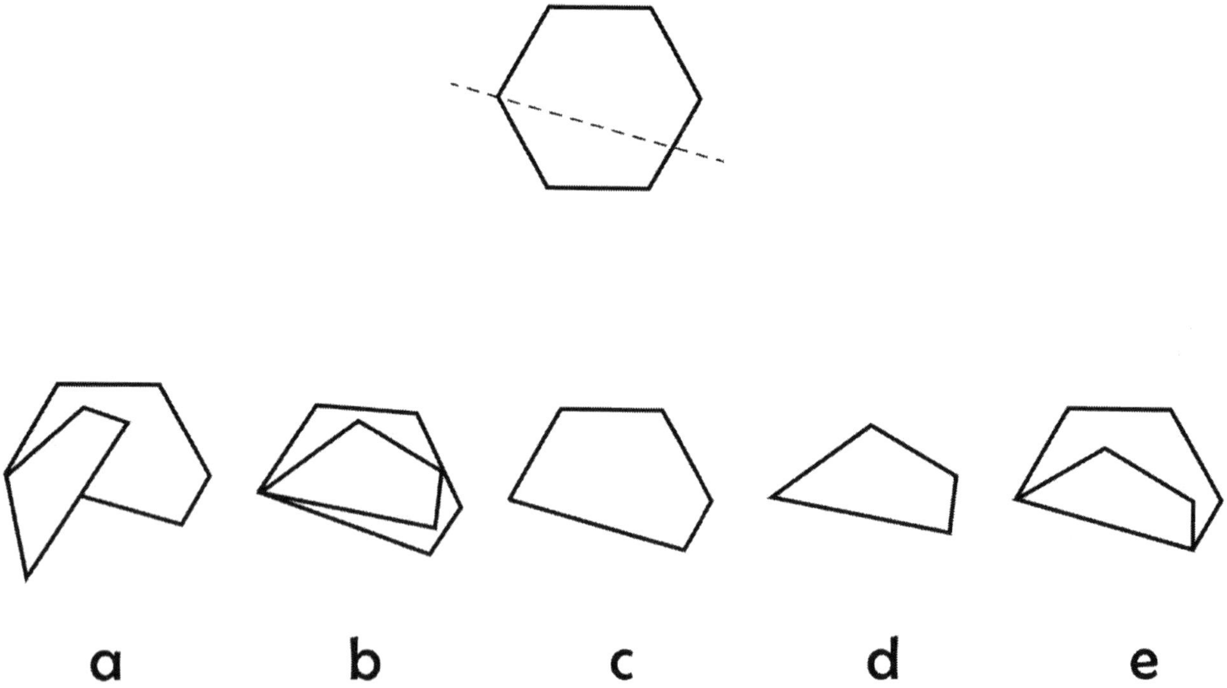

3.

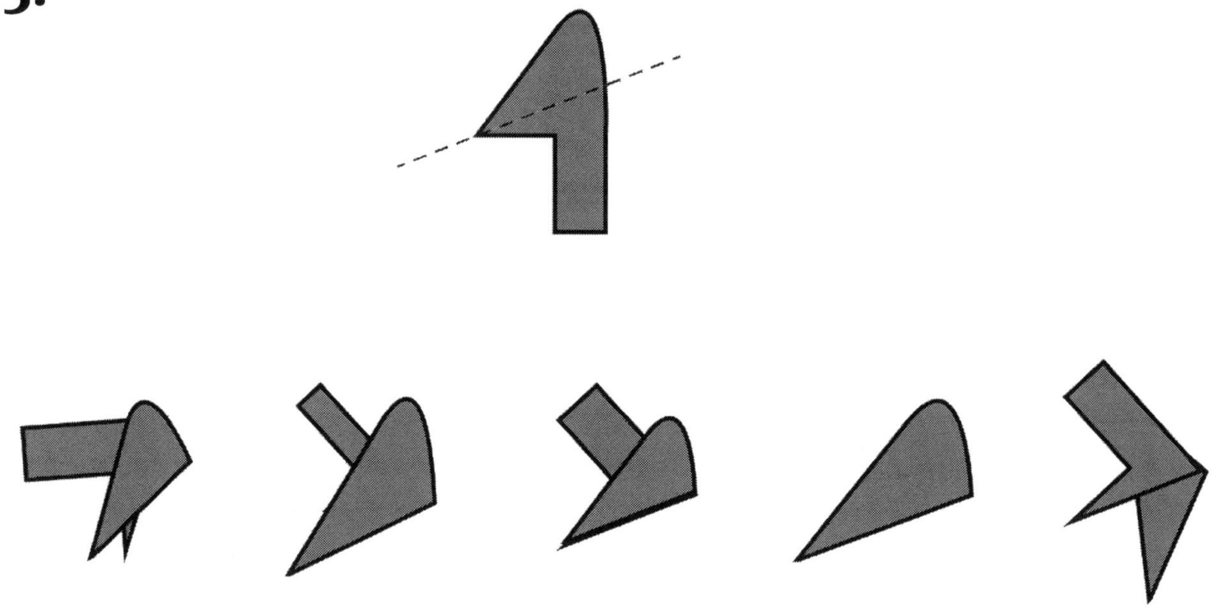

a b c d e

4.

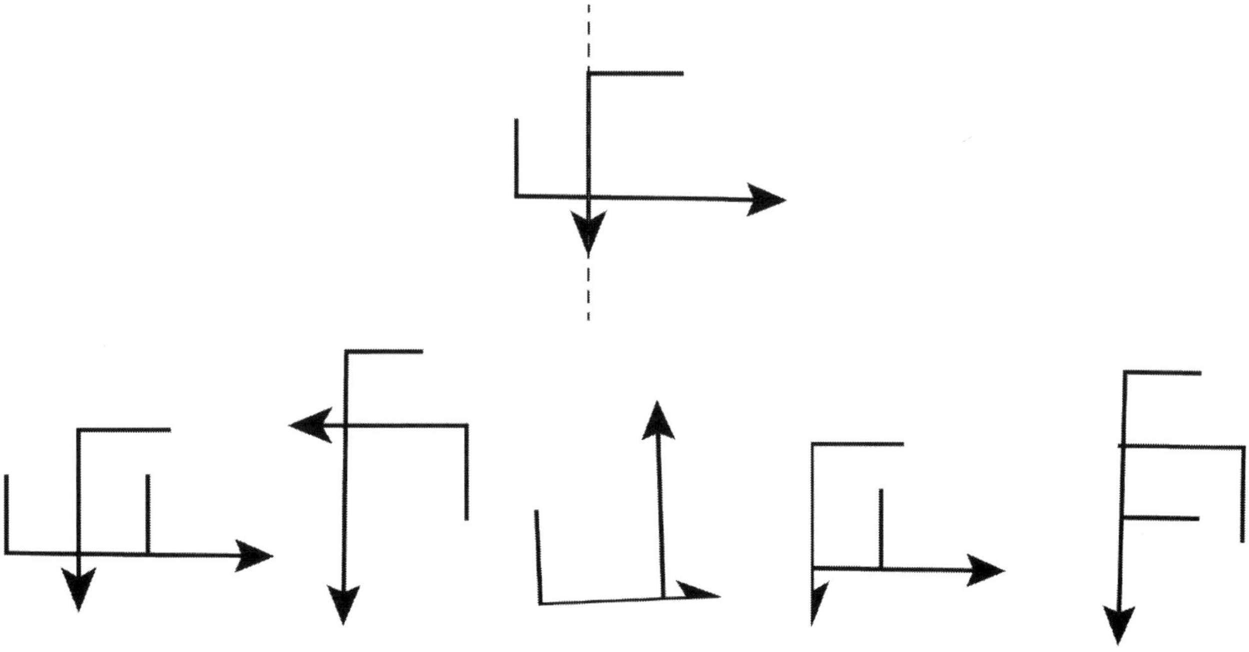

a b c d e

PLEASE TURN THE PAGE AND CONTINUE

5.

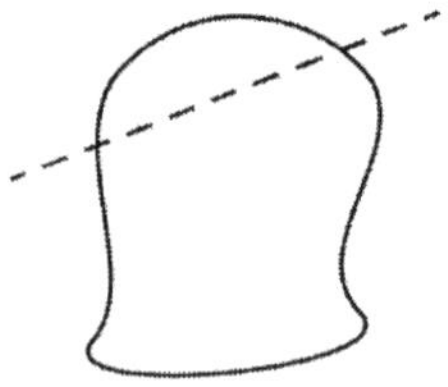

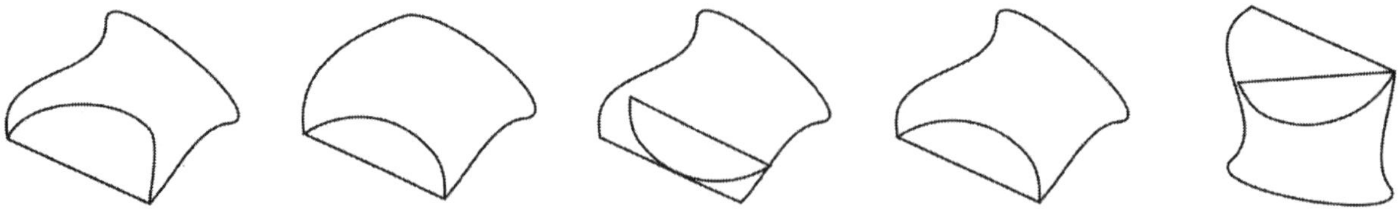

a b c d e

6.

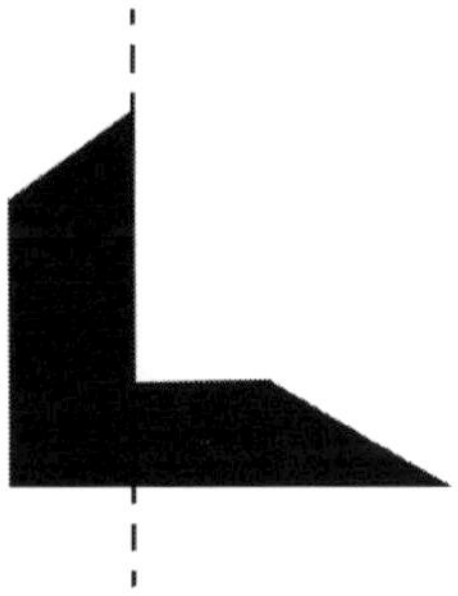

a b c d e

7.

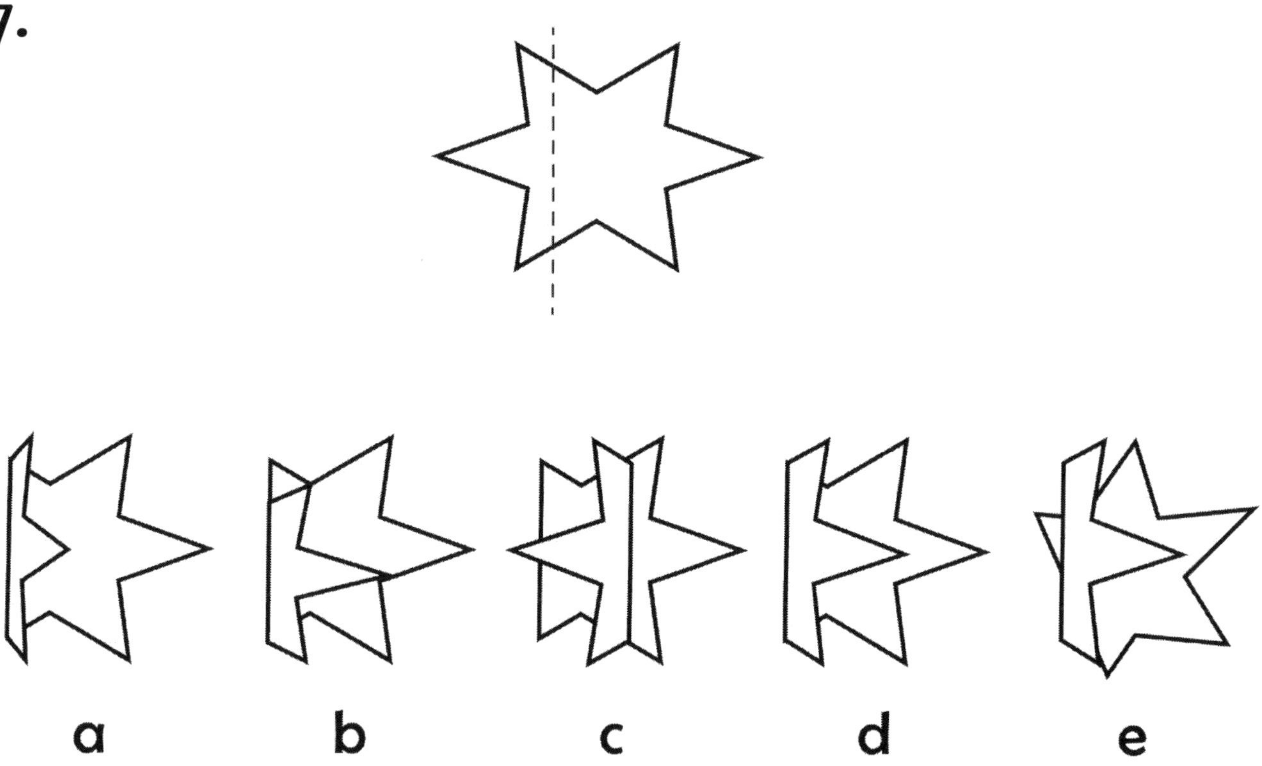

8.

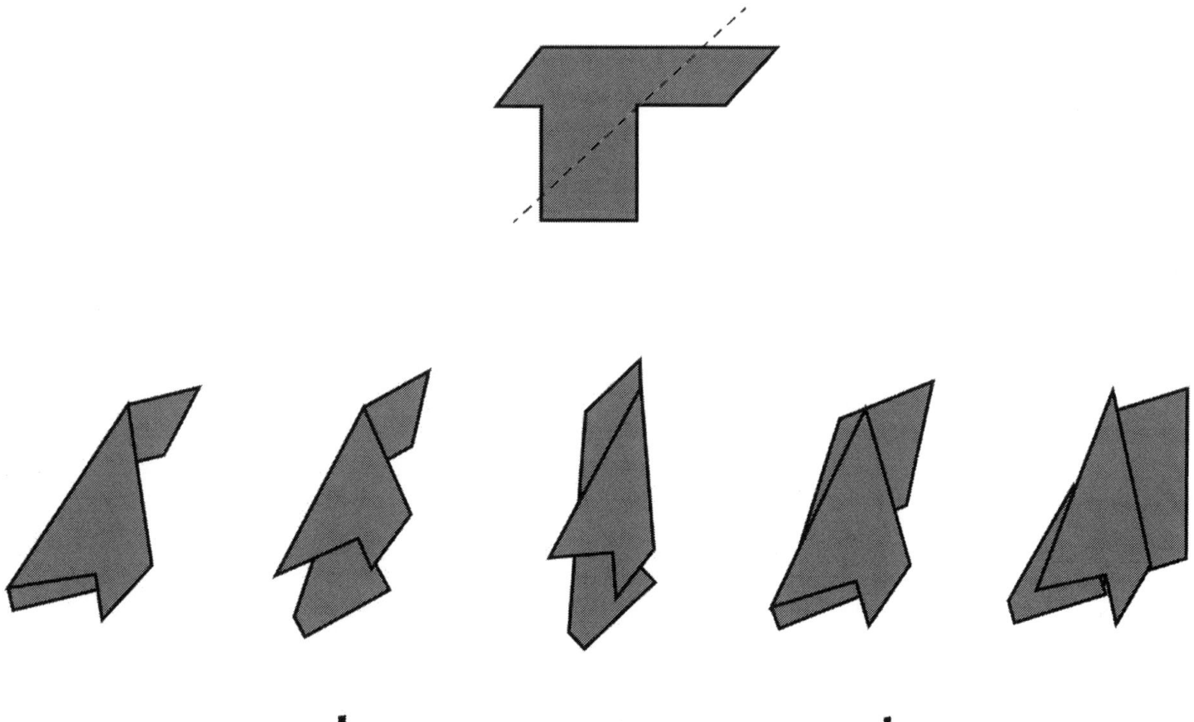

PLEASE TURN THE PAGE AND CONTINUE

9.

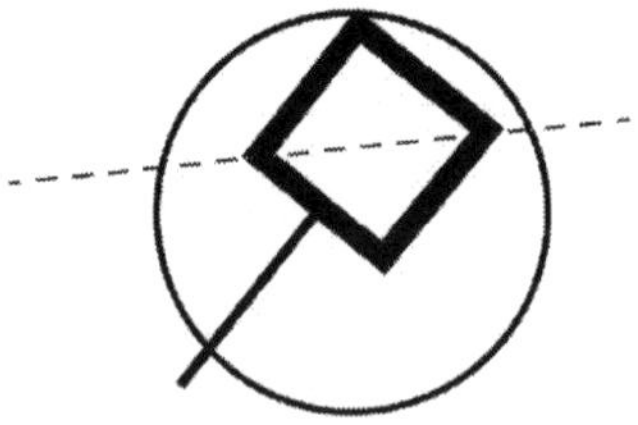

a b c d e

10.

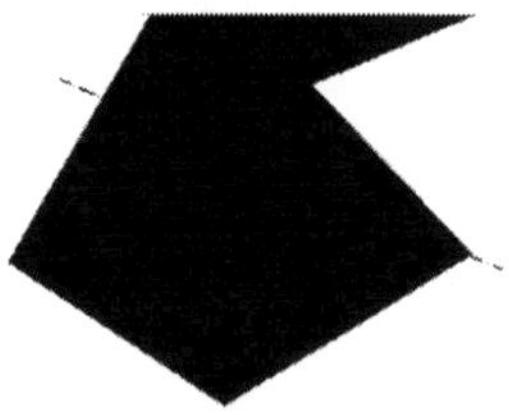

a b c d e

11.

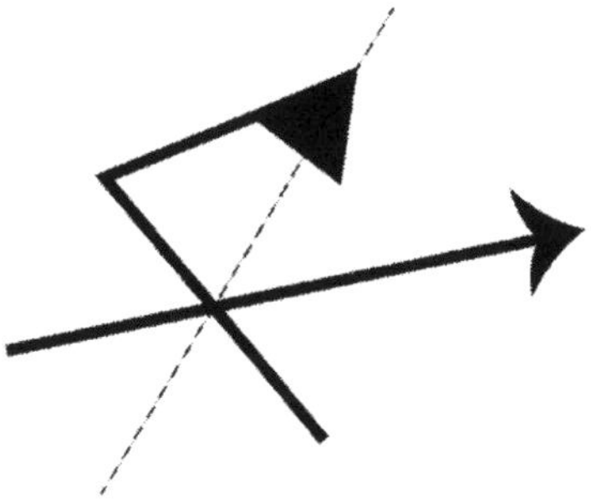

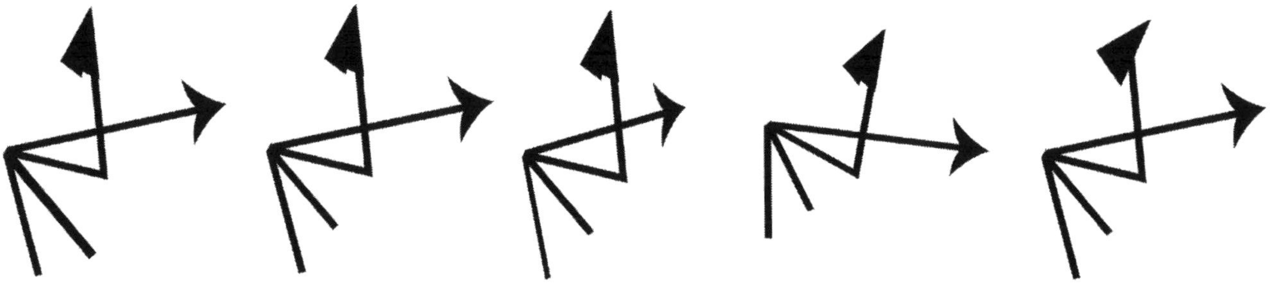

a b c d e

12.

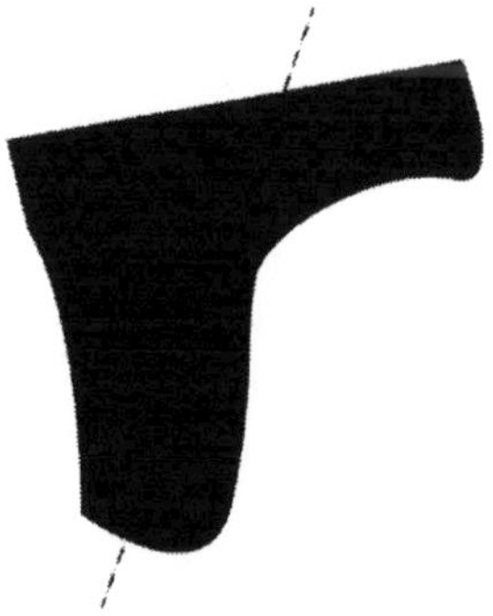

a b c d e

END OF SECTION 1 – PLEASE DO NOT TURN THE PAGE

Section 2 (Time allowed - 6 minutes)

Which picture can be made by combining the first two shapes?

Example:

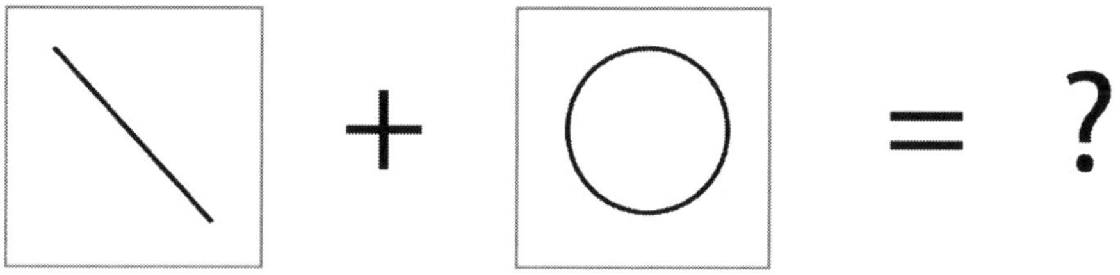

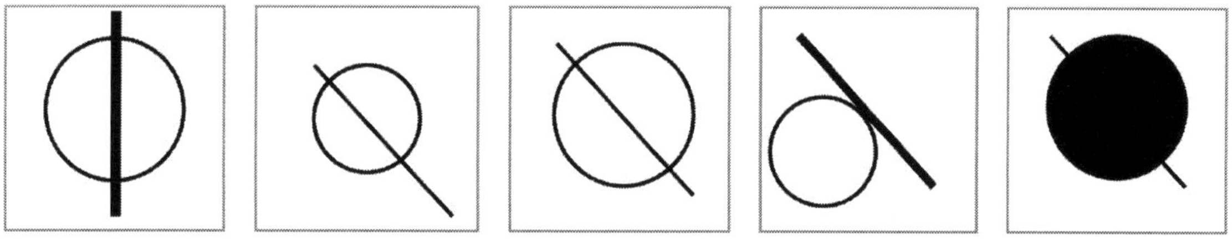

a b (c) d e

The correct answer is: **C**

PLEASE WAIT UNTIL YOU ARE ASKED TO TURN OVER

13.

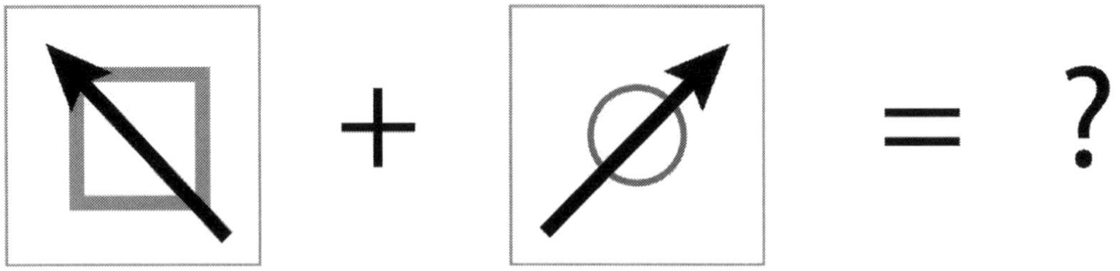

a b c d e

14.

a b c d e

15.

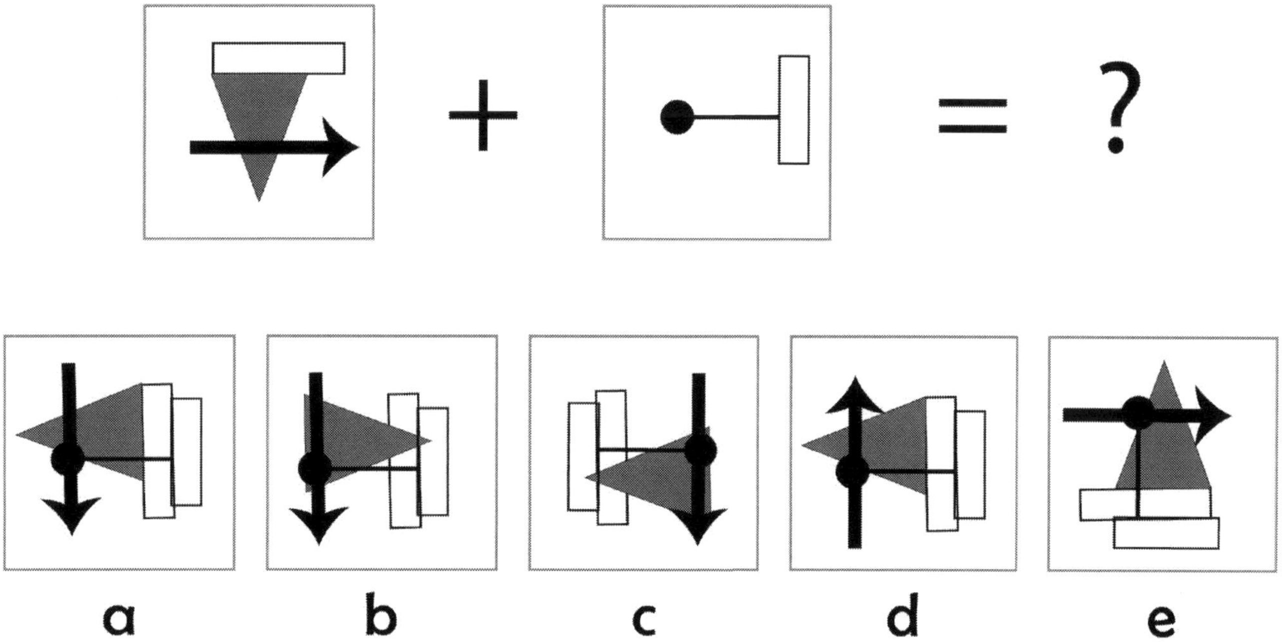

16.

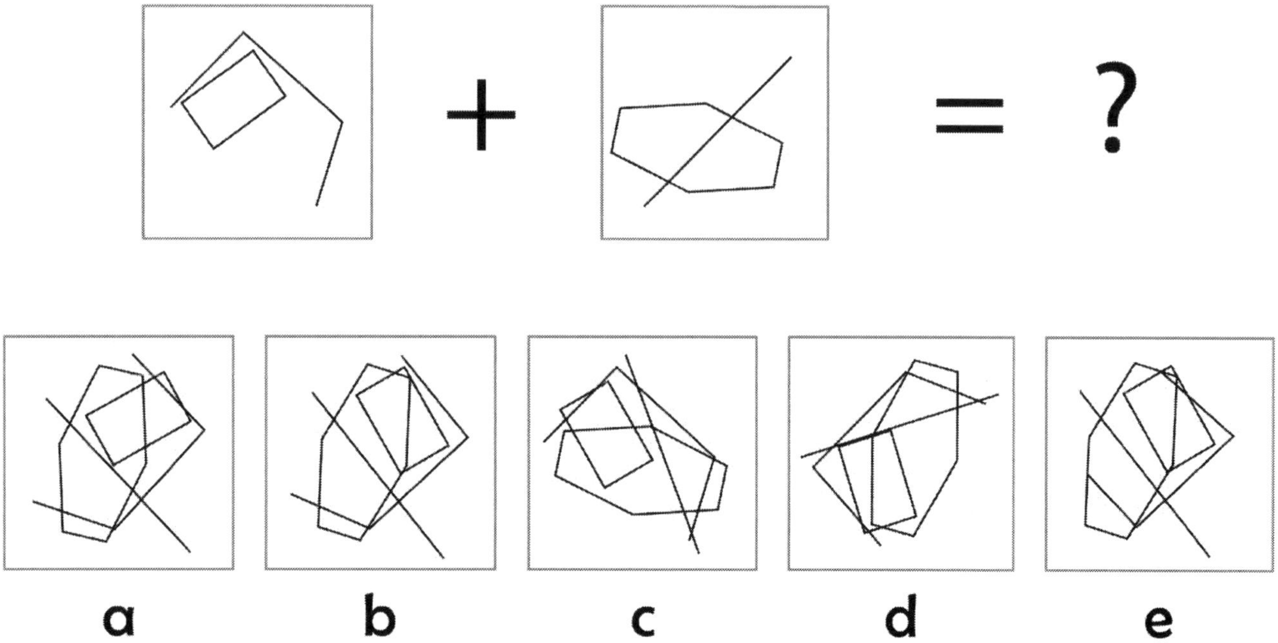

PLEASE TURN THE PAGE AND CONTINUE

17.

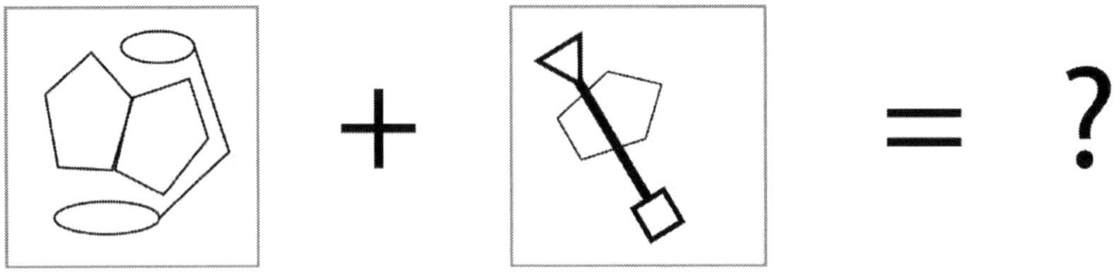

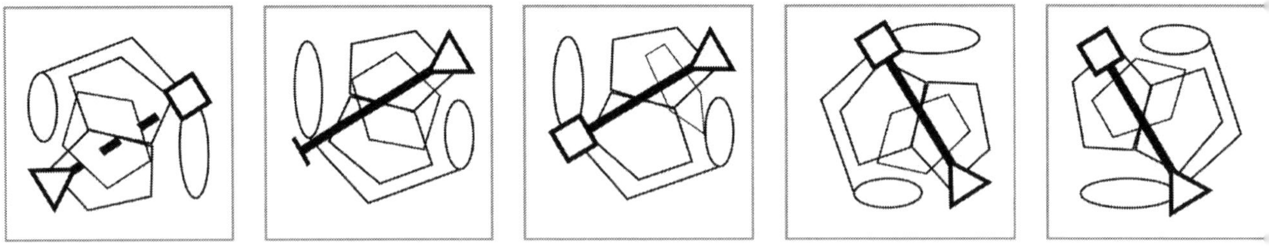

a b c d e

18.

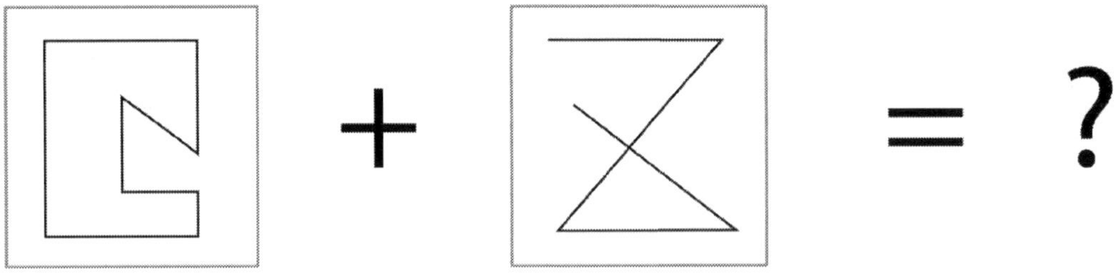

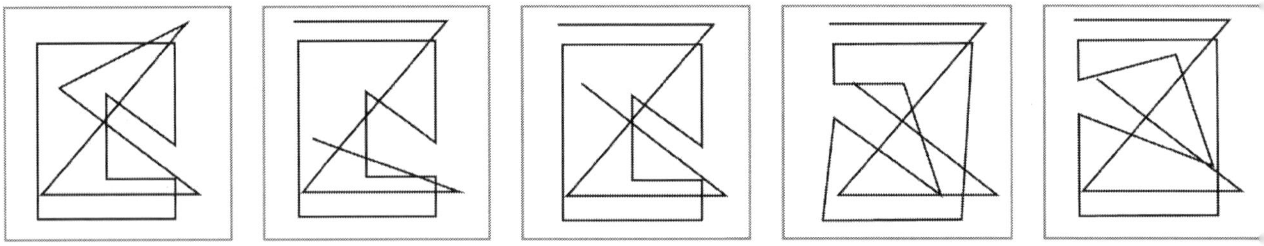

a b c d e

19.

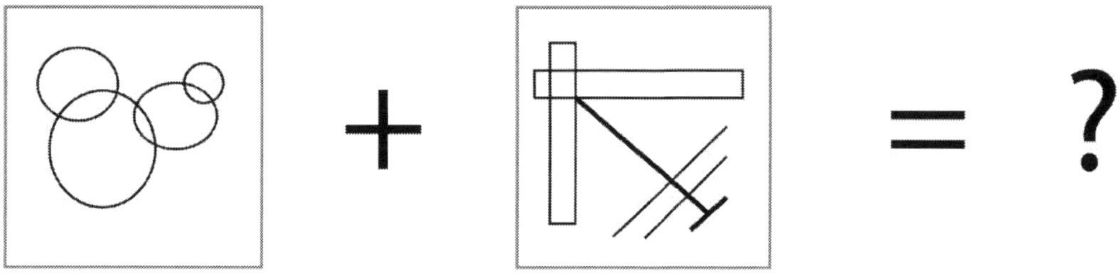

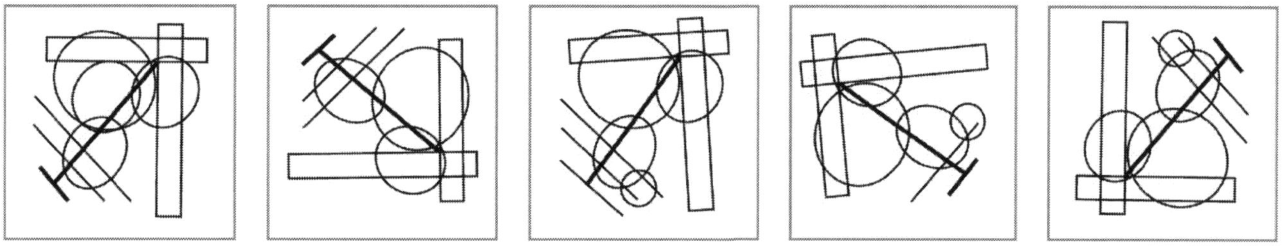

a b c d e

20.

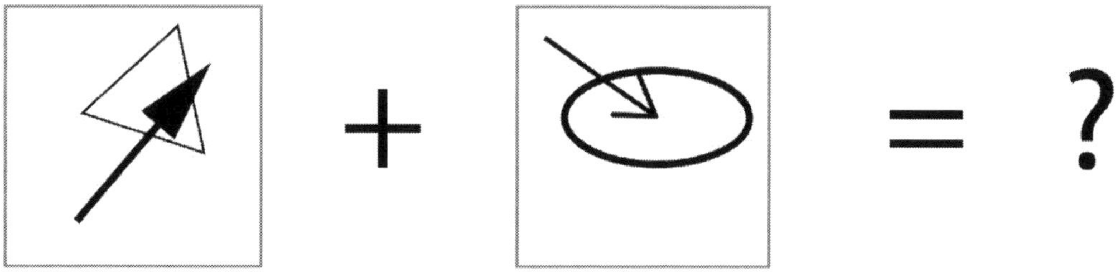

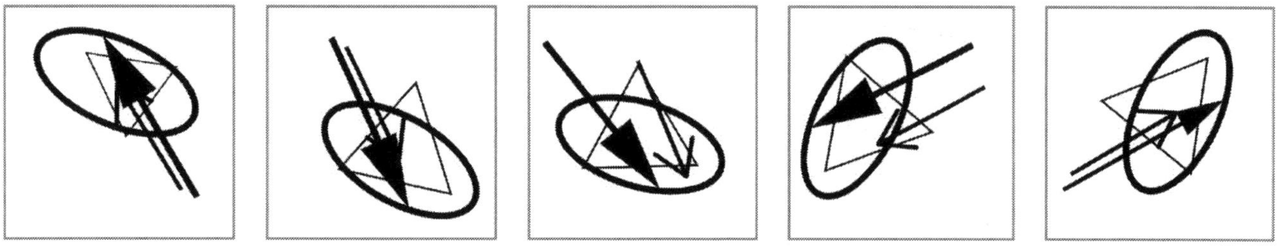

a b c d e

PLEASE TURN THE PAGE AND CONTINUE

21.

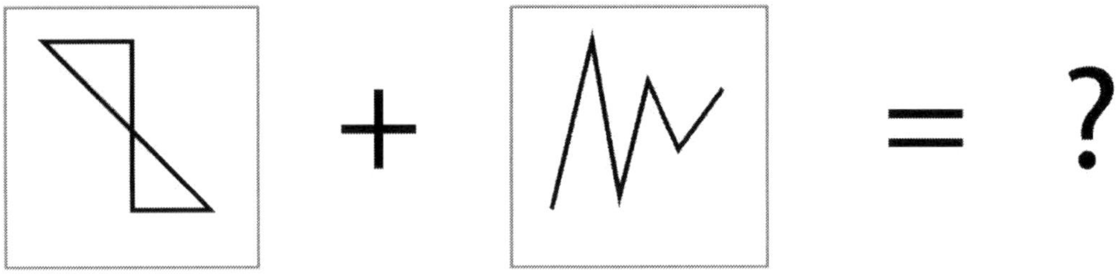

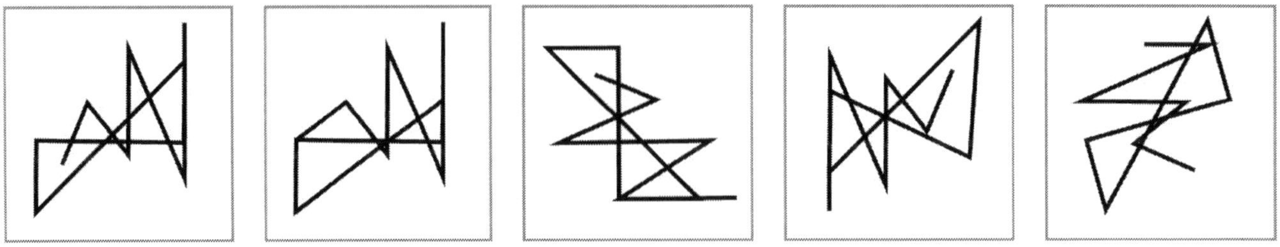

a b c d e

22.

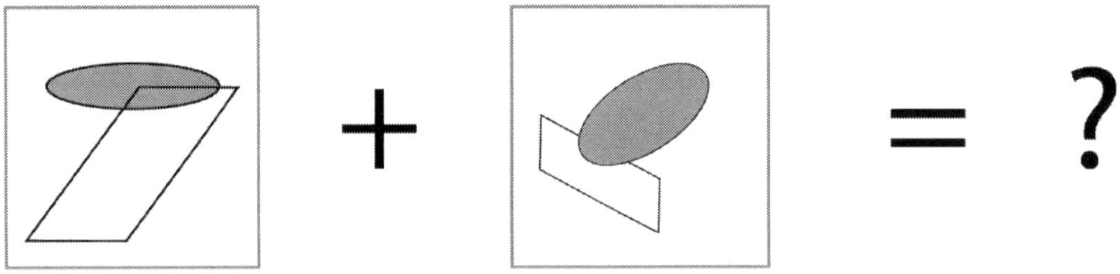

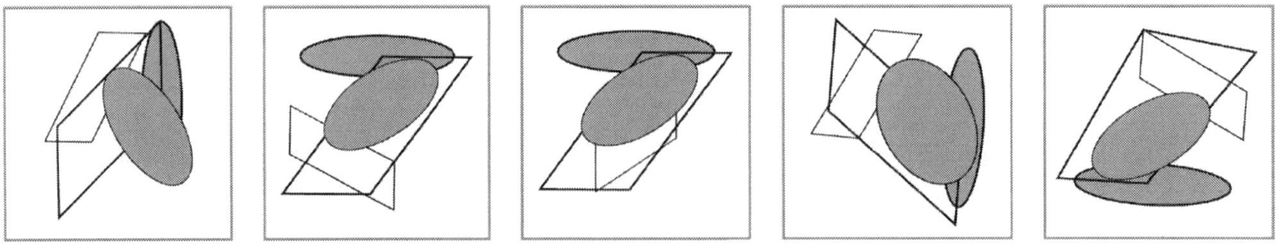

a b c d e

23.

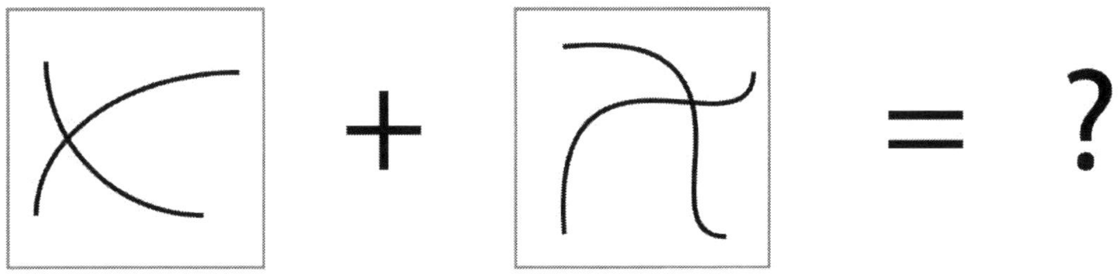

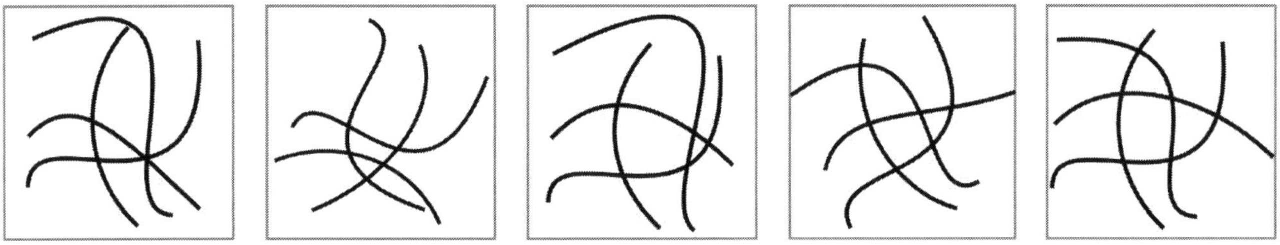

a b c d e

24.

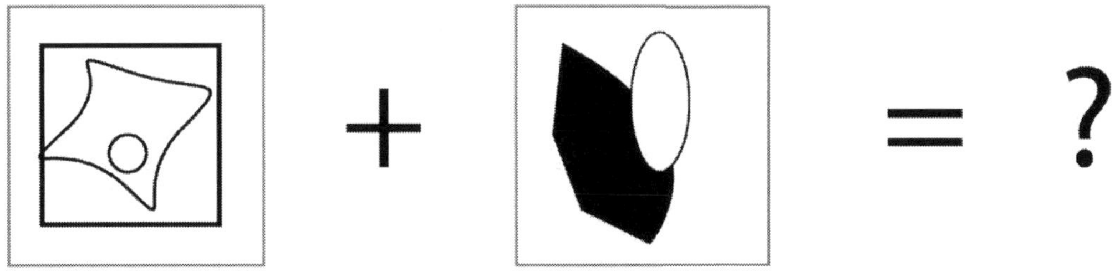

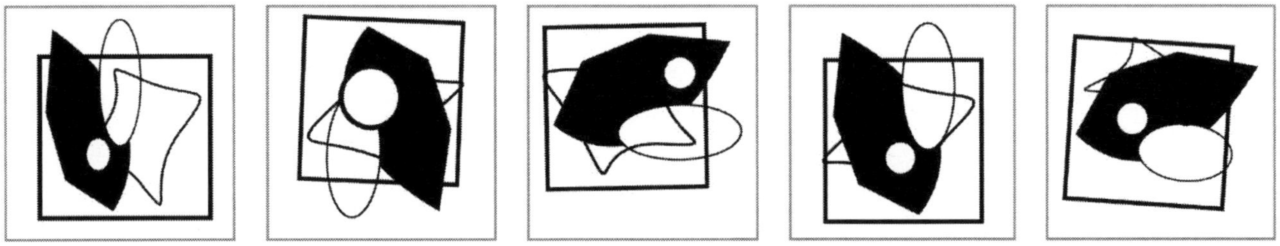

a b c d e

END OF SECTION 2 – PLEASE DO <u>NOT</u> TURN THE PAGE

Section 3 (Time allowed - 6 minutes)

In these questions, work out which of the five options best fits in the gap left in the top sequence.

Example:

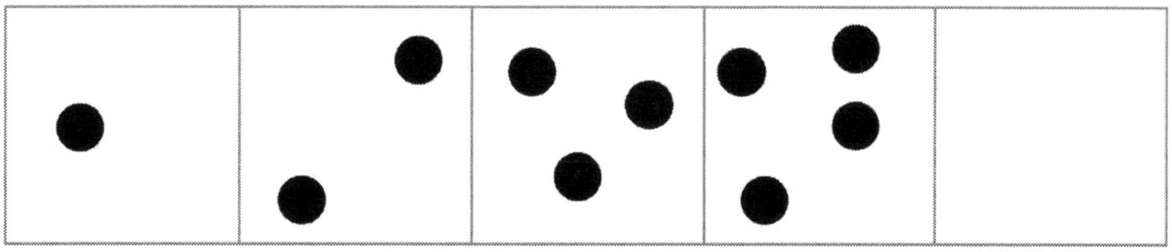

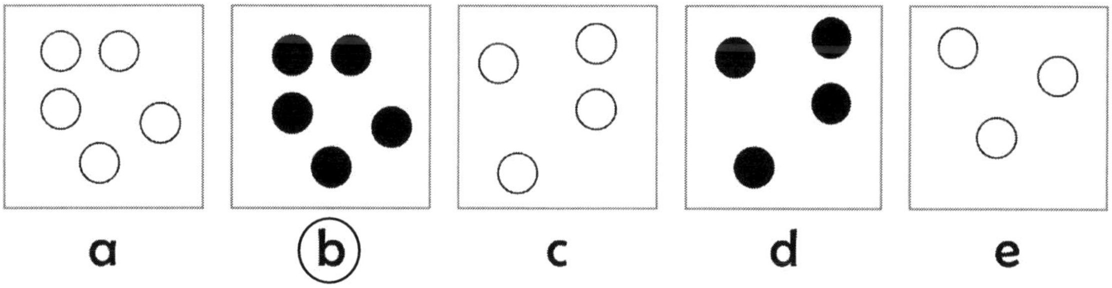

The correct answer is: **b** as this is the only option with five black dots.

PLEASE WAIT UNTIL YOU ARE ASKED TO TURN OVER

25.

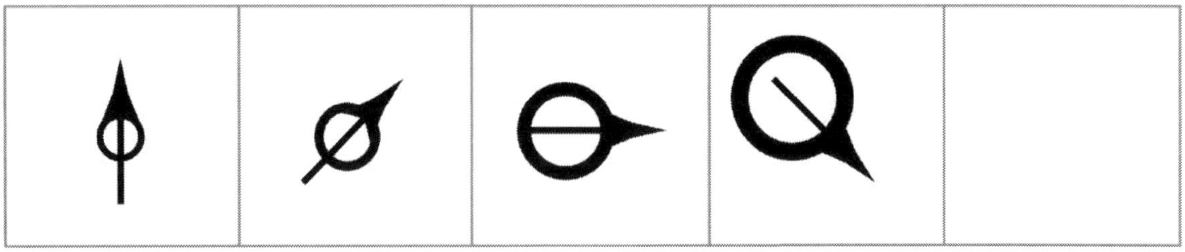

a b c d e

26.

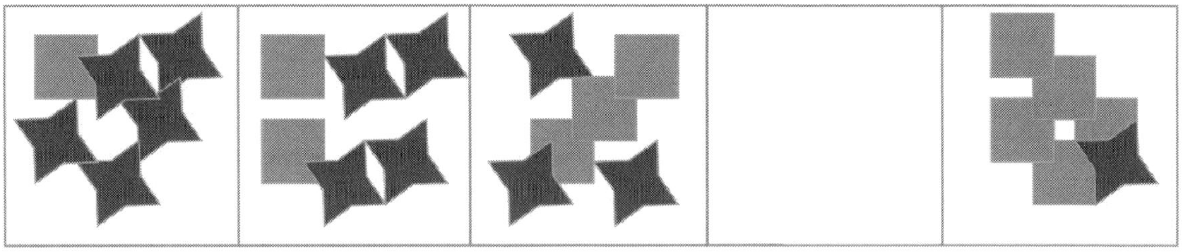

a b c d e

27.

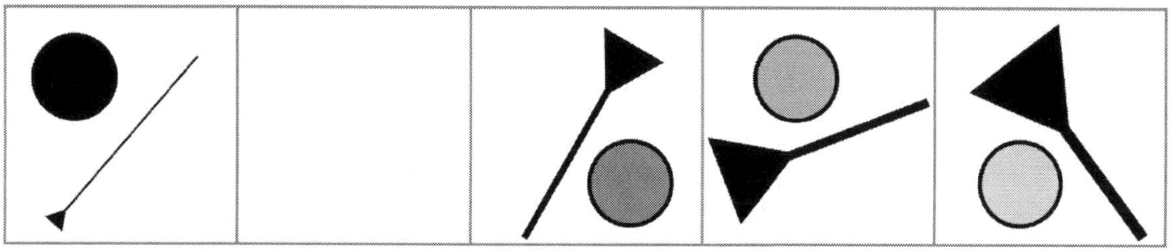

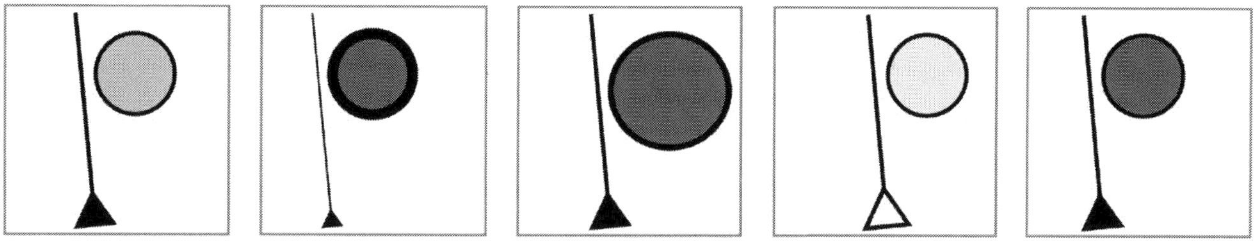

a b c d e

28.

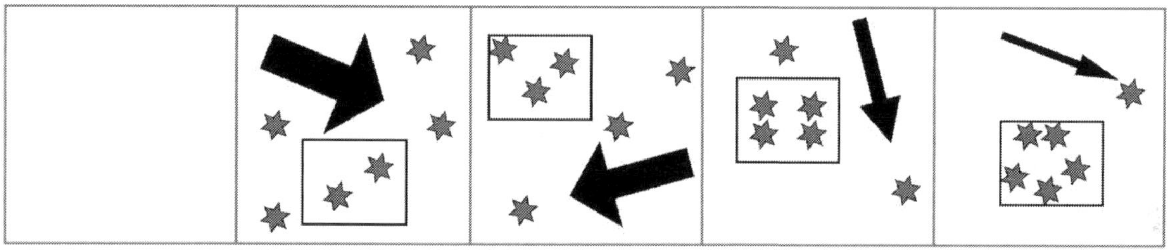

a b c d e

PLEASE TURN THE PAGE AND CONTINUE

29.

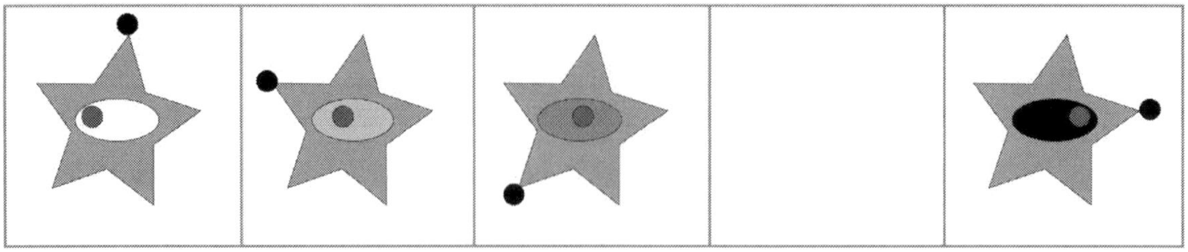

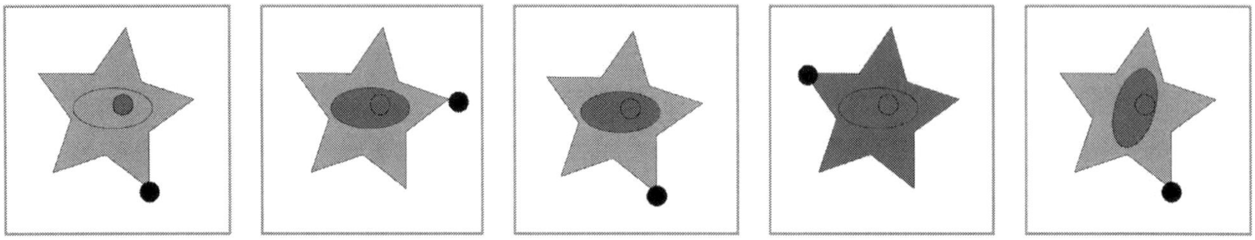

a b c d e

30.

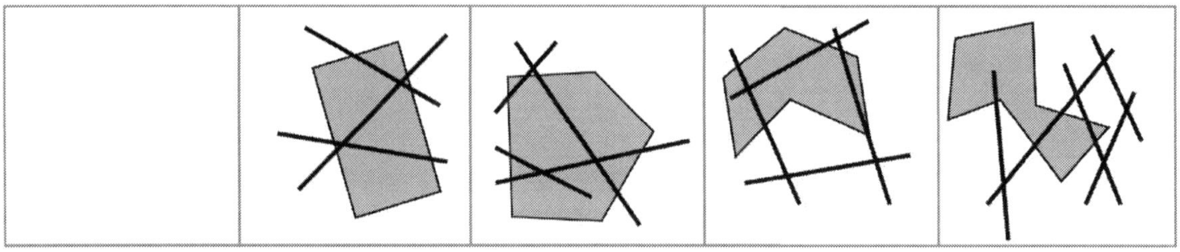

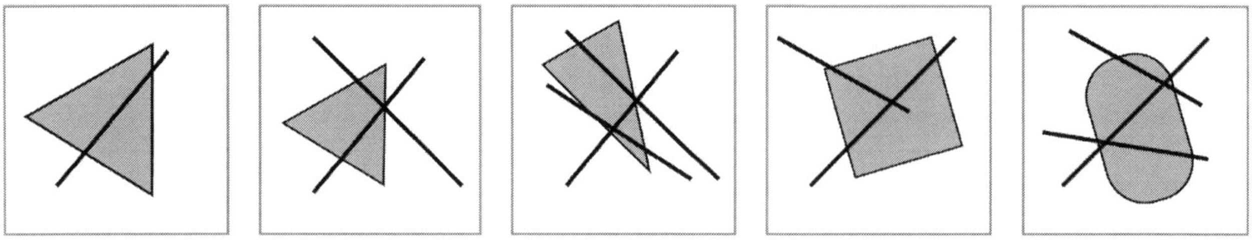

a b c d e

31.

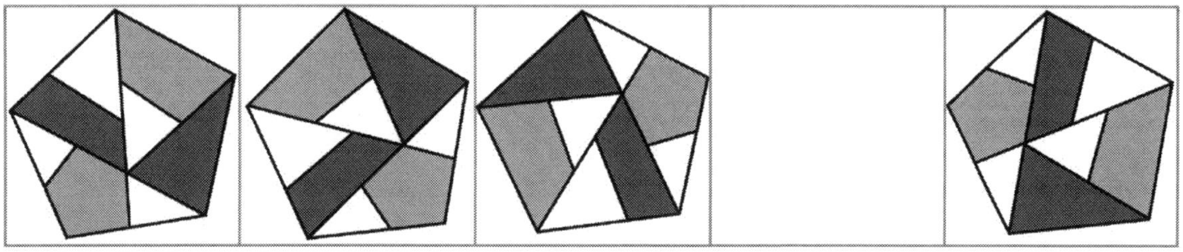

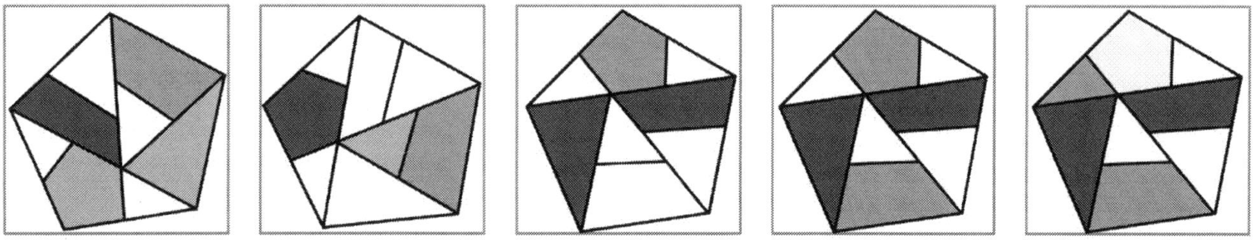

a b c d e

32.

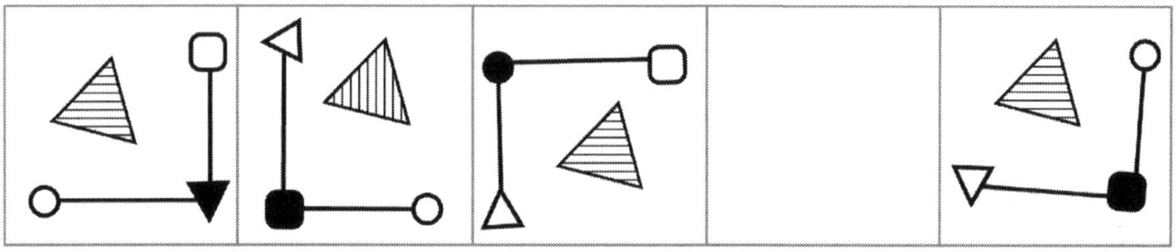

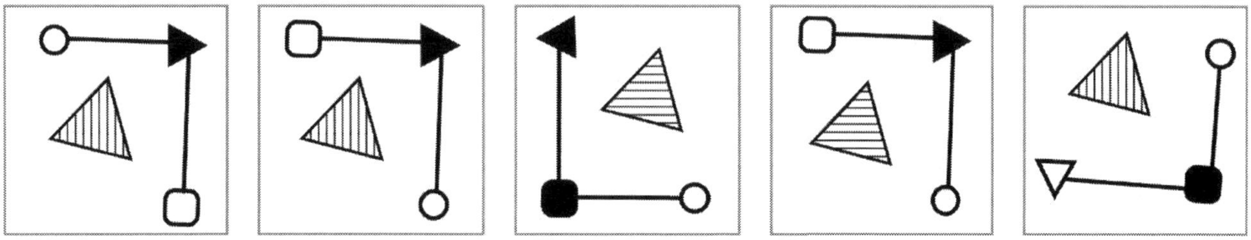

a b c d e

PLEASE TURN THE PAGE AND CONTINUE

33.

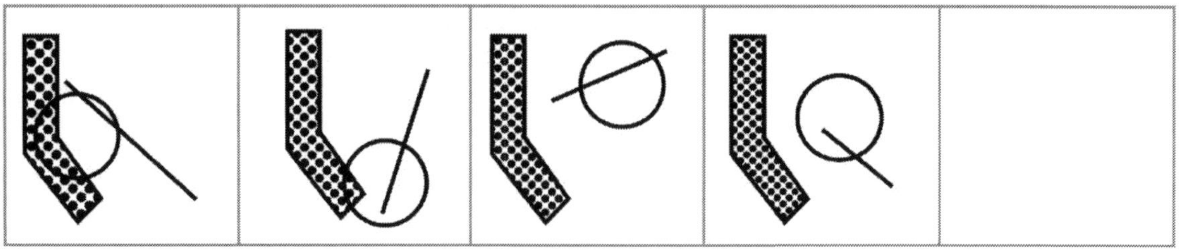

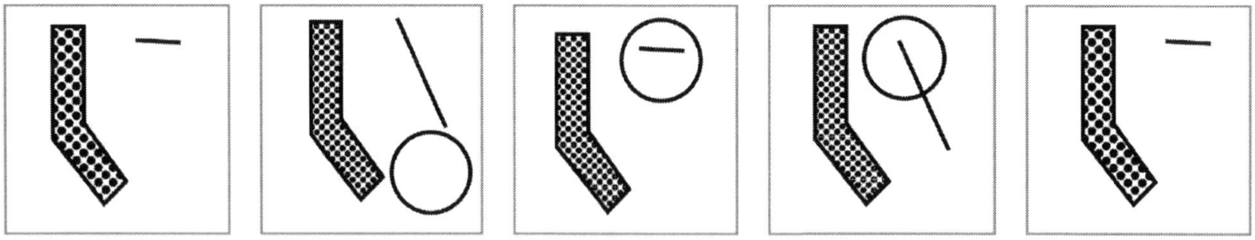

a b c d e

34.

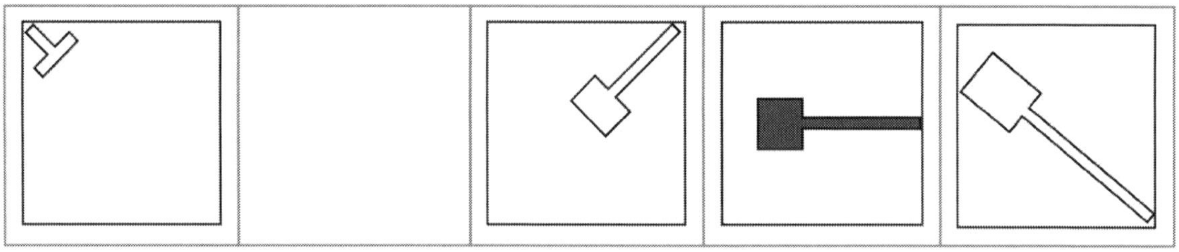

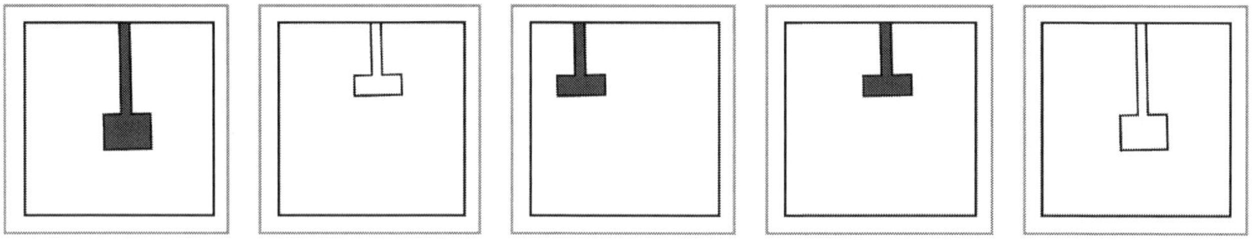

a b c d e

35.

a b c d e

36.

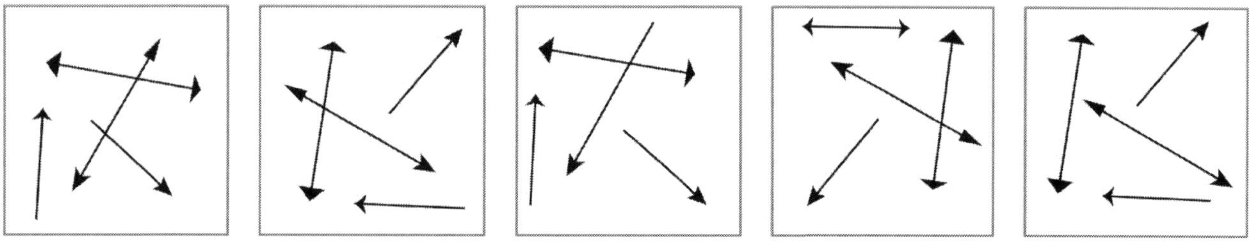

a b c d e

PLEASE TURN THE PAGE AND CONTINUE

Section 4 (Time allowed - 6 minutes)

For the next twelve questions, look at the relationship between the first and second shapes. Then look at the third shape and decide which of the options shows the same relationship from this shape.

Example:

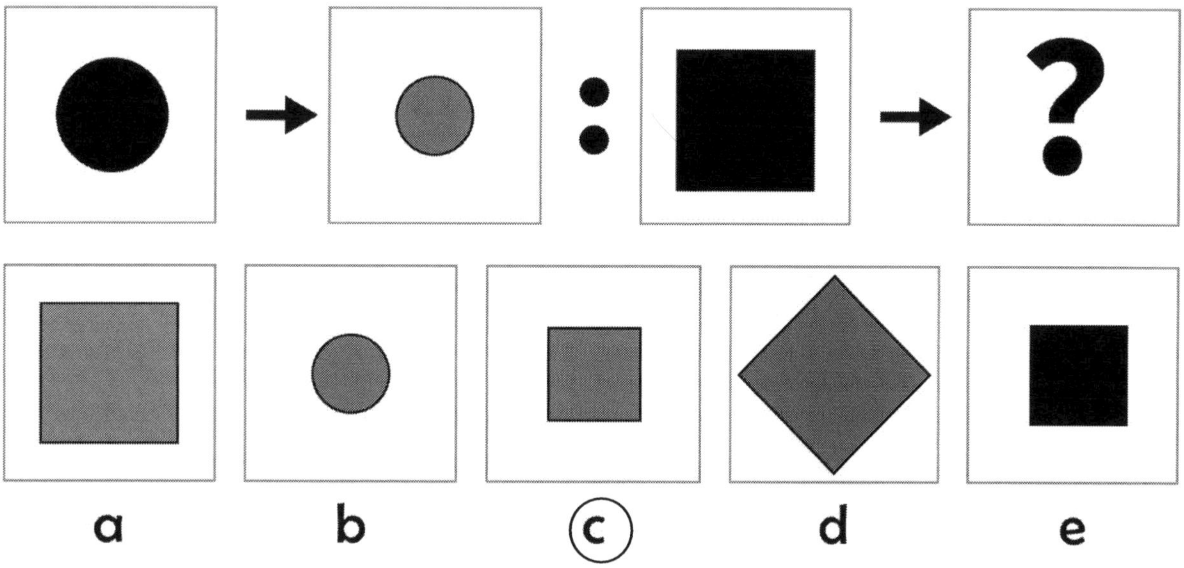

The correct answer is: **C**

The shape shrinks and turns from black to grey.

PLEASE WAIT UNTIL YOU ARE ASKED TO TURN OVER

37.

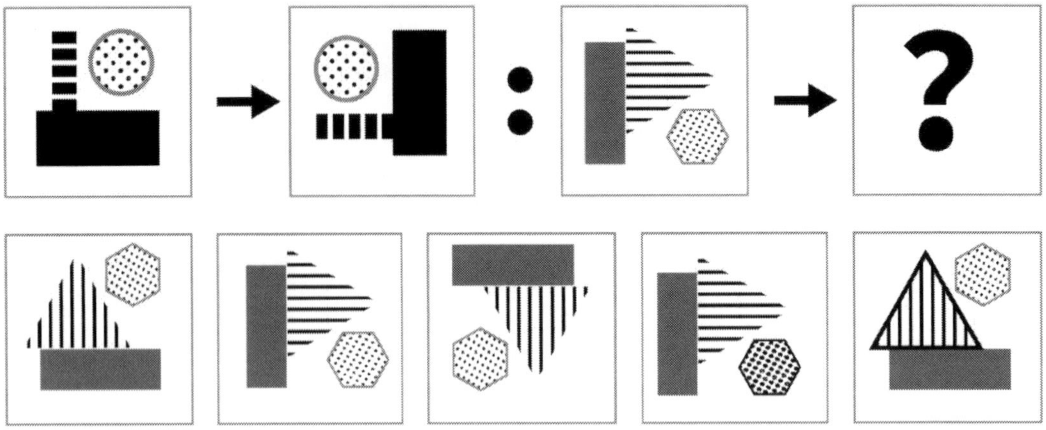

a b c d e

38.

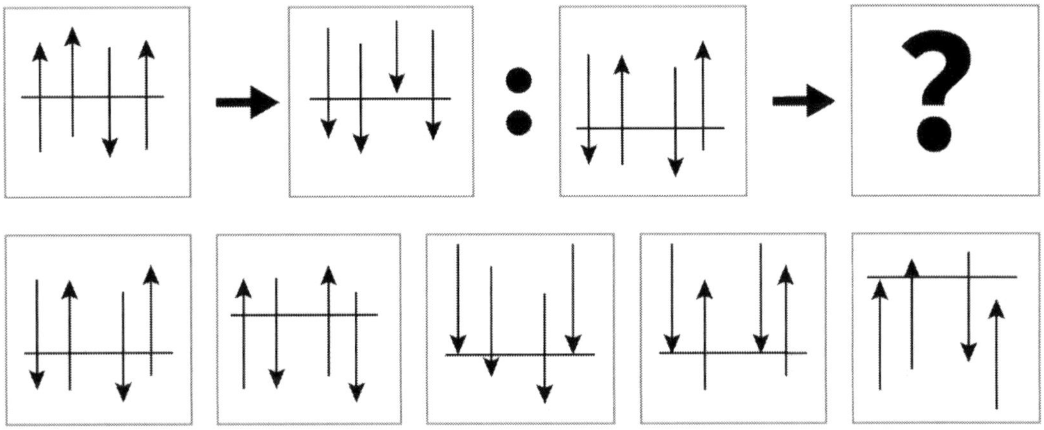

a b c d e

39.

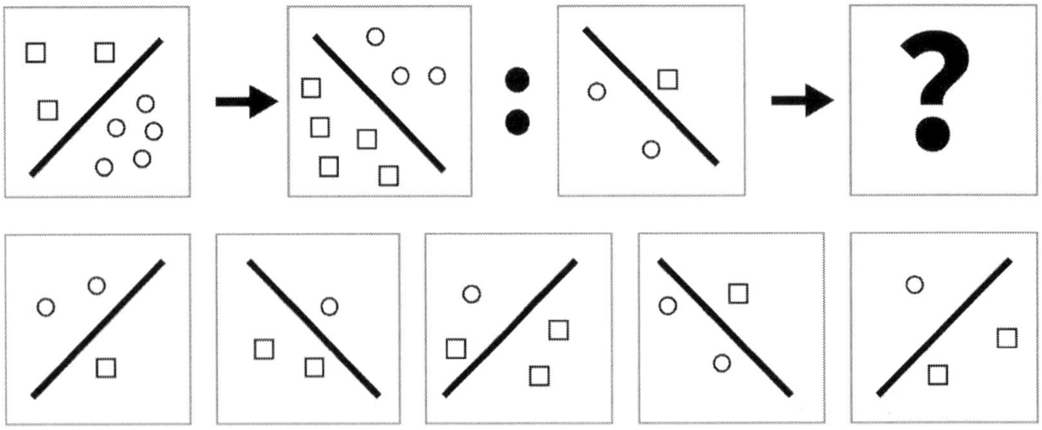

a b c d e

40.

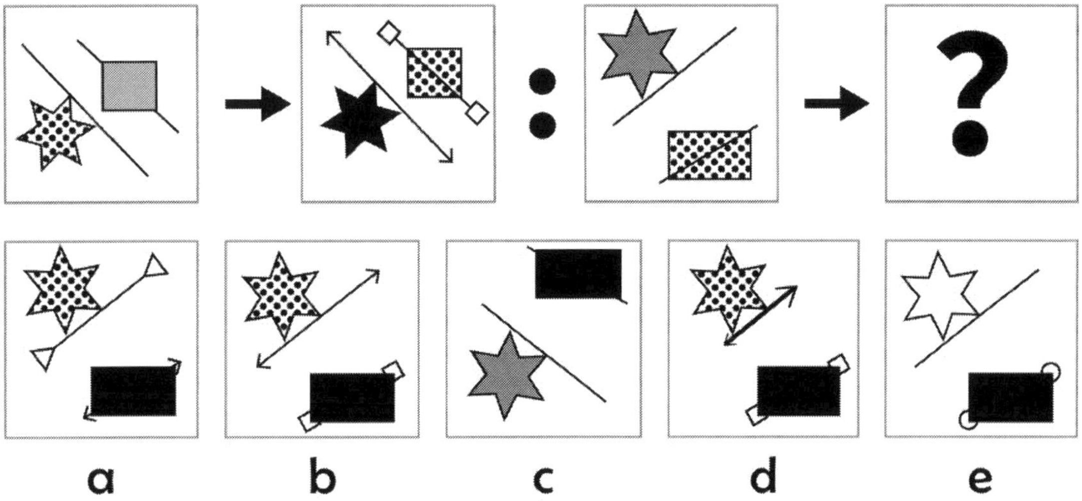

41.

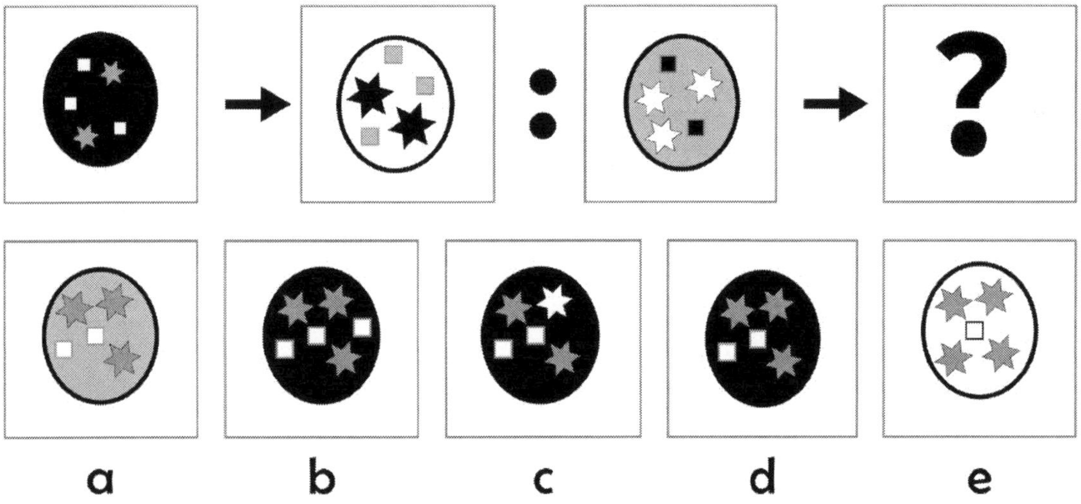

42.

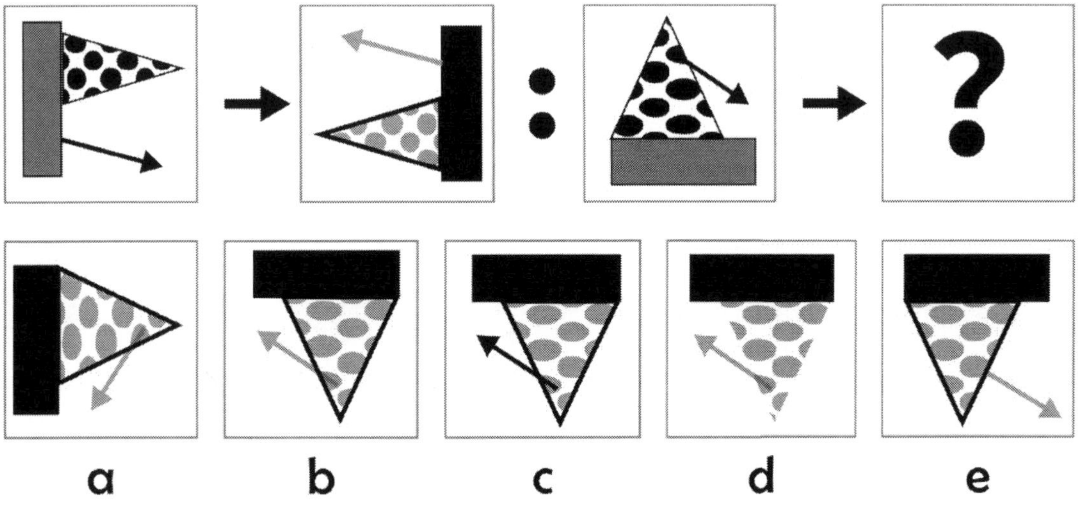

PLEASE TURN THE PAGE AND CONTINUE

43.

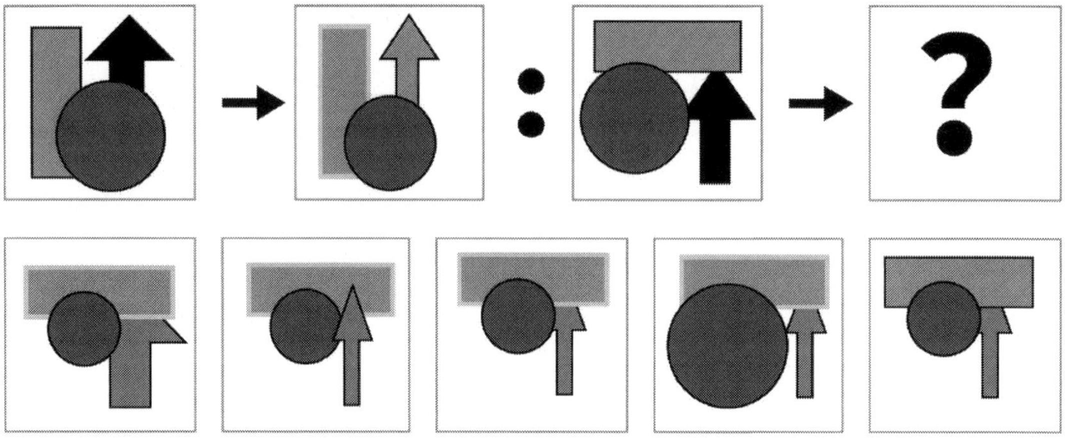

a b c d e

44.

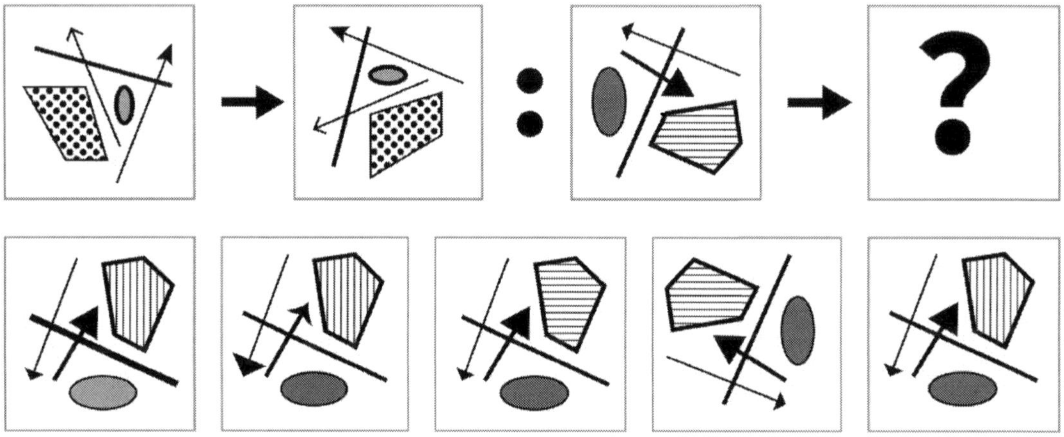

a b c d e

45.

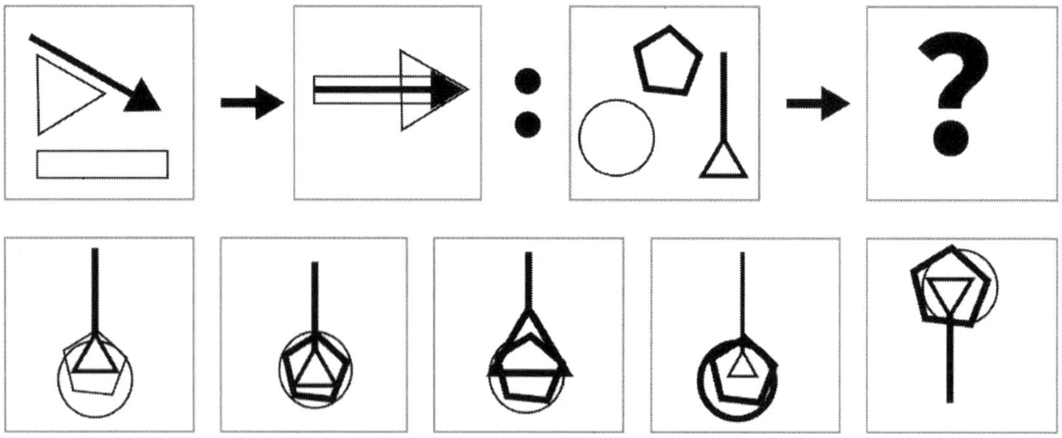

a b c d e

46.

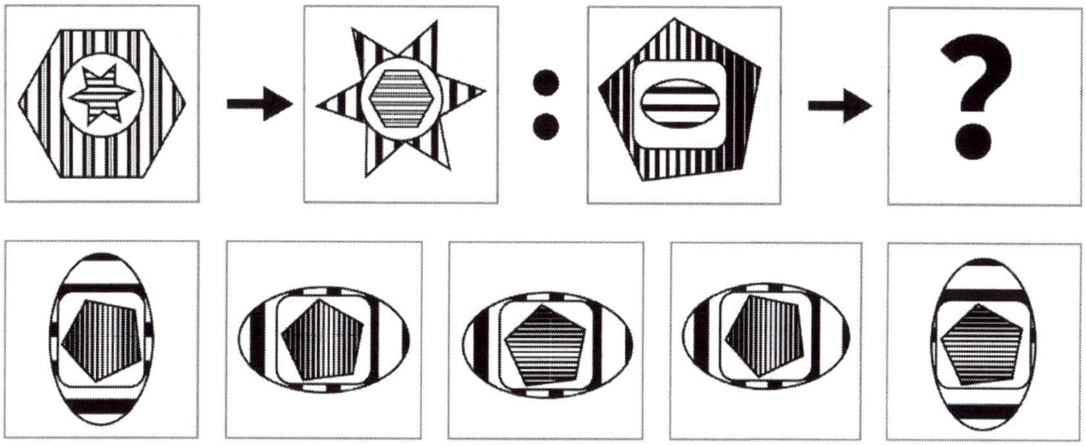

a b c d e

47.

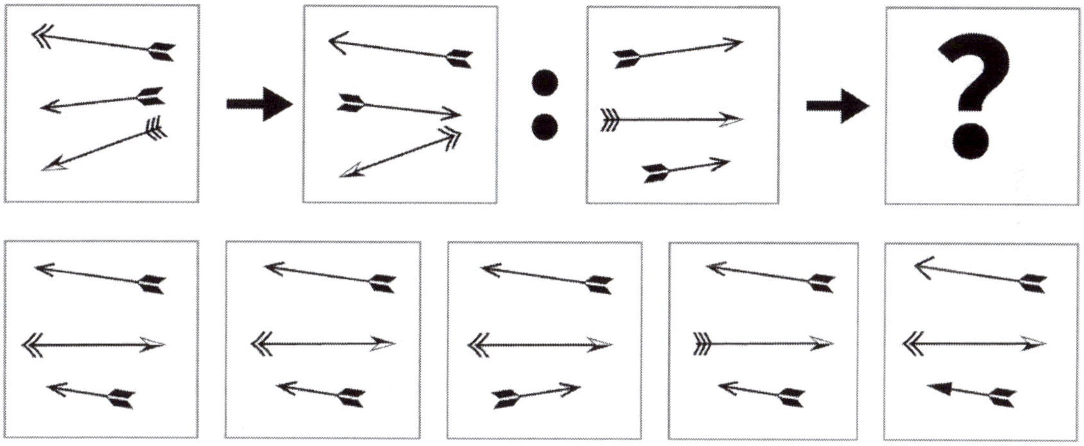

a b c d e

48.

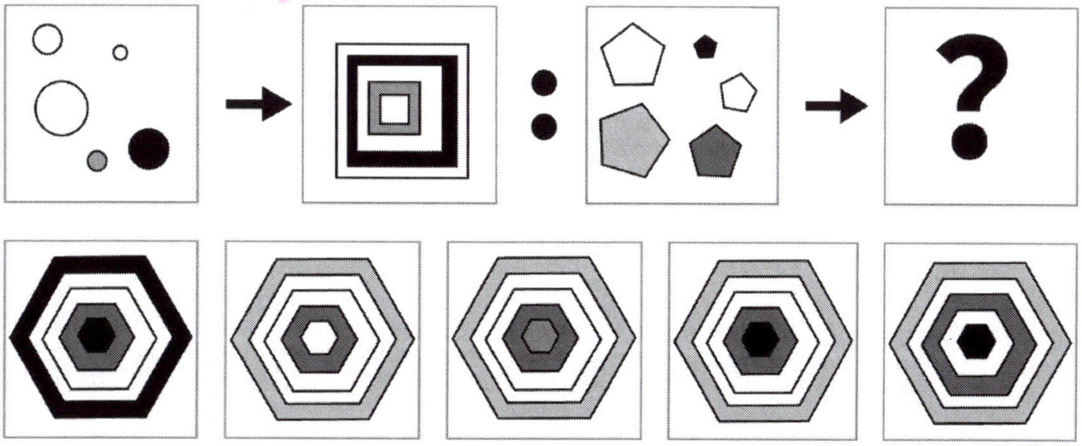

a b c d e

END OF SECTION 4

THE NON-VERBAL REASONING TEST IS COMPLETE

WRITING

Paper 2

Instructions

1. You will have a writing task explained to you.
2. Once the task has been explained, you will be given time to plan and write.
3. You will have 40 minutes to complete your writing; this includes 10 minutes planning time.

WRITING TASK: The Aliens Have Landed

Either

(a) Make up a short story about an alien spacecraft landing in your school playground. Are they friendly or do they cause trouble?

or

(b) Invent an alien species and describe these aliens in detail. What do they look like? How do they move? Do they make any sounds? Make your description as vivid as you can.

Use the space below to plan your writing.
Option chosen: a or **b** (please circle your choice)

Write your composition on this page.

THE TEST IS COMPLETE – PLEASE ASK FOR EXTRA PAPER IF NECESSARY.

ANSWERS

Maths Paper 1

1. **C** 27059
2. **B** 8
   If ¾ = 60 then ÷3 to get ¼ = 20;
   The number is 20 x 4 = 80;
   a tenth of 80 is 8.
3. **B** two (23 and 29 are prime)
4. **A** 7627
   263 x 10 = 2630;
   263 x 20 = 5260 (double 2630);
   263 x 30 = 5260 + 2630 = 7890;
   263 x 29 = 7890 – 263 = 7627
5. **E** 480
   15 x ((2 x 12) + 8) = 15 x (24 + 8)
   = 15 x 32;
   10 x 32 = 320;
   5 x 32 = 160 (half 320);
   15 x 32 = 320 + 160 = 480
6. **B** 210cm^2
   Area = ½ x base x height
   = ½ x 21 x 20
   = (½ x 20) x 21
   = 10 x 21 = 210
7. **A** 255
   4 x 60 = 240, 0.25 = ¼;
   ¼ of 60 = 15;
   240 + 15 = 255
8. **D** $\frac{5}{16}$
   Total ingredients: 250+280+230+40 = 800;
   Fraction sugar = $\frac{250}{800} = \frac{25}{80} = \frac{5}{16}$
9. **B** 150, 500
   area is 7,525,000 ÷ 50
   = 752500 ÷ 5 = 150,500
10. **D** 132.963
11. **D** 60
    20% is 12;
    100% is 5 x 12 = 60
12. **A** £57.75
    165 x 5 = 1650 ÷ 2 = 825;
    825 papers x 7p = 5775p;
    5775p = £57.75
13. **A** 17
    range = highest – lowest
    = 84 – 67 = 17
14. **C** 1 hour
    graph horizontal between 1300 and 1400
15. **A** 2
    Inverse operations:
    78 ÷ 2 = 39;
    39 – 23 = 16;
    16 ÷ 8 = 2
16. **D** 500,000mm
    ½km = 500m;
    500m = 50,000cm (x100);
    50,000cm = 500,000mm (x10)
17. **D** 133
    +2, +4, +8, +16, +32, ...+64;
    69 + 64 = 133
18. **B** 30°
    23 - - 7 = 23 + 7 = 30
19. **D** 15.5
    12 + 19 = 31;
    31 ÷ 2 = 15.5
20. **C** 37.5%
    $\frac{1}{4}$ = 25%, $\frac{1}{8}$ = 12.5%;
    $\frac{3}{8} = \frac{1}{4} + \frac{1}{8}$ = 25 + 12.5 = 37.5
21. **C** £12812.50
    12,500 ÷ 10 = 1250 (10%);
    1250 ÷ 2 = 625 (5%);
    625 ÷ 2 = 312.50 (2.5%);
    12,500 + 312.50 = 12812.50
22. **B** 10th May
    20th April – 240;
    30th April – 480 (ten days later);
    10th May – 960 (ten days later)
23. **E** 250
    5 is prime, 25 = 5^2, 125 = 5^3;
    216 = 6 x 6 x 6 = 6^3
24. **B** 1340
    15 + 35 = 50 mins;
    2.30pm – 1 hour = 1:30pm;
    1:30pm + 10mins = 1:40pm = 1340
25. **C** £10.80
    10% of £12.00 = £1.20;
    £12.00 - £1.20 = £10.80

English Paper 1

1. **C** two (too cold/too dark)
2. **B** parentheses (brackets)
3. **B** terrible thing that will happen
4. **A** rang a bell (*A bell rang)*
5. **B** empty
   an *idle threat* is an *empty threat*
6. **E** neglected
   pondered = considered/thought about;
   neglected = did not consider
7. **A** nonsense (*a nonsensical explanation)*
8. **C** the police would have been called
   (...*not worried enough to call the police*)
9. **B** entity
   e.g. an alien being = a strange entity
10. **C** immodest
    immodest = boastful
    (e.g. *Marie-Anne's idea was...*
    brilliantly amazingly fantastic)
11. **A** *like baby bear's porridge*
    a simile compares something with
    something else
12. **D** ambles
    sauntered = ambled = walked slowly
13. **E** daisys
    should be *daisies*
14. **A** Presumabely
    should be *Presumably*
15. **N** no error
16. **B** would
    should be *wood* (homophone)
17. **B** similer
    correct spelling = similar
18. **B** comma not needed
19. **B** should be a full stop
20. **D** colon is incorrect here
21. **N** no error
22. **E** should be a ?
23. **D** catalogued (made a mental list)
24. **B** became
25. **A** row (not *shelf* as this is repetition)
26. **B** their
27. **E** exact (*middle* is tautology)
28. **B** six and a half (brackets give extra information)
29. **E** to her knowledge (sub. clause)
30. **A** incongruous (odd/inconsistent)

VR Paper 1

Section 1

1. **A** alert & **Y** negligent
alert (v.) = vigilant
negligent (v.) = inattentive

2. **C** bruise & **Y** heal
bruise (v.) = hurt
heal (v.) = make better

3. **A** superfluous & **Z** vital
superfluous (adj.) = unessential
vital (adj.) = essential

4. **A** dispense & **Y** keep
dispense (v.) = distribute
keep (v.) = retain

5. **B** unorthodox & **Z** mainstream
unorthodox (adj.) = unconventional
mainstream (adj.) = ordinary

6. **A** cease & **Z** inaugurate
cease (v.) = stop
inaugurate (v.) = start

7. **A** succumb & **Y** withstand
succumb (v.) = surrender
withstand (v.) = endure

Section 2

8. **B** considered items *edit*
9. **A** leave illegal *veil*
10. **B** its pancake *span*
11. **D** spin to *pint*
12. **C** who offered *hoof*
13. **B** hardly related *lyre*
14. **A** criticism ugly *smug*
15. **C** cars Americans *same*
16. **C** eight hours
Monday – 90 mins
Tuesday – 0 mins (lesson)
Wednesday – 90 mins
Thursday – 90 mins
Friday – 90 mins
Weekend – 2 hours
Monday – 0 mins (exam)
90 x 4 = 360mins (6 hours)
6 + 2 hours = 8 hours

Section 3

17. **D** 43
+4, +5, +6...?... +7, +8
? = 37 + 6 = 43

18. **A** 32
add previous two numbers
4 + 8 = 12; 8 + 12 = 20;
12 + 20 = 32

19. **B** 81
square numbers descending
or +11, +13, +15, +17 (R to Left)

20. **D** 240
x2, x3, x4, x5
48 x 5 = 240

21. **B** 110
(R to L) +1.25, +2.5 (doubled)
+5, +10; 100 + 10 = 110

22. **B** 16
numbers double
(powers of 2) 8 x 2 = 16

23. **E** 582
+110
472 + 110 = 582

24. **B** 296
+5, +10, +15, +20, +25...
291 + 5 = 296

25. **C** 198.5
+100, +50 (halved), +25
+12.5; 186 + 12.5 = 198.5

26. **B** 1
x3, x4, x5, x6
inverse: 3 ÷ 3 = 1

27. **B** 18
double sequence;
odd terms: 6, 12, ? (+6)
even: 12, 24, 36 (+12)
12 + 6 = 18

Section 4

28. **B** XZ
first letters H,L,P,T,? +4
second letters J,N,R,V,? +4
T + 4 = X; V + 4 = Z; XZ

29. **D** OM
(+3, -3);
L + 3 = O; P – 3 = M; OM

30. **A** QV
first (+2, +3, +4, +5);
second (+2, +3, +4, +5);
L + 5 = Q; Q + 5 = V; QV

31. **D** JM
(+2, -3);
H + 2 = J; P – 3 = M; JM

32. **E** KL
first (+1, +2, +3, +4);
second (+2, +3, +4, +5);
G + 4 = K; G + 5 = L; KL

33. **B** YK
(-1, +2);
Z – 1 = Y; I + 2 = K; YK

34. **C** BQ
(+5, -5);
W + 5 = B; V – 5 = Q; BQ

35. **B** CN
first (-1, +2, -3, +4);
second (-12, +11, -10, +9);
Y + 4 = C; E + 9 = N; CN

36. **E** JO
first (-1, -2, -3, -4);
second (+5, +4, +3, +2);
N – 4 = J; M + 2 = O; JO

Section 5

37. **C** y
play, year, stay, yard

38. **A** l
foil, lisp, hurl, lute

39. **C** w
gnaw, wane, flew, line

40. **E** e
true, ever, tree, easy

41. **B** e
vane, east, cone, edge

42. **A** h
posh, hail, bath, hoax

43. **D** y
fray, your, ally, yoke

44. **D** b
numb, bile, comb, brie

Section 6

45. **C** content
content = gratified
content = what it contains

46. **D** desert
desert = punishment
e.g. *they received their just deserts*
(they deserved to be punished)
desert = to abandon
e.g. to desert a sinking ship

47. **A** refuse
refuse = rubbish
e.g. there was a pile of refuse
refuse = to choose not do something
e.g. I refuse to do that

VR Paper 1 cont.

48. **E** wind
wind (rhymes with binned) = gust or breeze
e.g. the cold wind blew
wind (rhymes with lined) = turn
e.g. a winding road = road with lots of turns

49. **B** minute
min<u>ute</u> = very small
e.g. the insect was minute
<u>min</u>ute = small amount of time
e.g. I'll be there in a minute

50. **A** project
project = a task
e.g. they worked on the project together
project = to throw
e.g. project a missile

51. **E** compound
compound = having several parts
e.g. a compound noun
compound = a mixture
e.g. a compound of sodium and chlorine

52. **C** 1.15p.m.
45 mins + 10 mins + 20 mins = 75 mins
75mins + 5 mins (needs to be 5 mins early)
=80 mins = 1 hour 20 mins;
1435 = 2.35p.m.;
2.35p.m. – 1 hour = 1.35 p.m.;
1.35p.m. – 20mins = 1.15p.m.

Section 7

53. **A** ANT
INCONSIST**ANT**

54. **C** SUM
CON**SUM**E

55. **A** BIT
INHA**BIT**ANTS

56. **E** LAD
MA**LAD**Y (illness)

57. **D** CAR
PRE**CAR**IOUS (dangerous)

58. **B** TOO
S**TOO**P (bend)

59. **C** PEN
SUS**PEN**D

60. **E** HER
AD**HER**E (stick)

61. **B** CAN
VA**CAN**T (empty)

Section 8

62. **B** & **X**
no+thing = nothing

63. **A** & **Z**
intent+ion = intention

64. **A** & **Y**
home+ward = homeward

65. **B** & **Z**
honey+dew = honeydew

66. **A** & **Z**
up+on = upon

67. **A** & **X**
hers+elf = herself

68. **C** & **X**
form+at = format

69. **B** & **Z**
pin+stripe = pinstripe
(pinstripe = dark cloth with narrow lines)
e.g. he wore a pinstripe suit

Section 9

70. **B** OQQP
each letter +2
e.g. C -> E, R -> T
MOON -> OQQP

71. **E** MSJXZL
-1, -2, -3...
e.g. R -> Q (-1) and A -> Y(-2) etc.
NUMBER -> M(-1), S(-2),J(-3) etc.

72. **C** £!*@+&=#
B = &, I = *, S = £, T = @
SUITABLE -> £..*@..&....
Despite not knowing all the letters,
the only possible choice is C.

73. **A** XUttS
each letters +5
e.g. R -> W (+5)
vowels in the word are lower case in the code;
e.g. I -> n

74. **B** RATES
C = 3 (count forwards from A);
R = 9 (count backwards from Z);
E = 5 (count forwards from A) etc.
A = 26, T = 20, E = 22;
Reverse this process with the given code;
18 = R (count 18 letters forward from A) etc.
26 = A, 20 = T, 22 = E, 19 = S -> RATES

Section 10

75. **B** 27
$9\,(12 \div 4) = 9 \times 3 = 27$

76. **B** 2
$14 \div (13 - (3 \times 2)) = 14 \div (13 - 6) =$
$14 \div 7 = 2$

77. **D** 8
$2\,(2 + 4 + 4 - 6) = 2 \times 4 = 8$

78. **A** ½
$\left(\frac{1}{2} + \frac{1}{4} + \frac{3}{4}\right) \div (3 \times 1) = 1\frac{1}{2} \div 3 = \frac{1}{2}$

79. **C** 84
$100 - (84 \div 7 \div 0.5) + 8$
$= 100 - (12 \div \frac{1}{2}) + 8$
$= 100 - 24 + 8 = 76 + 8 = 84$

80. **C** 0
(D – D) = 0
Any number multiplied by zero is zero so no need to work out second brackets.

NVR Paper 1

Section 1

1. **b**
all have three connected straight lines and an equal number of squares on each side

2. **d**
all have a rectangle and an upwards pointing arrow which crosses the rectangle once;
the border of rectangle **e** is too thick

3. **c**
all outer shapes are quadrilaterals and they all contain a fully enclosed circle;
the dots of shape **e** are too small

4. **e**
all contain two perpendicular matching arrows and one star with horizontal lines

5. **b**
all have rotational symmetry

6. **a**
all have one curved line and an arrow which crosses it, pointing to one small circle

7. **d**
all have white lines with the same spacing

8. **c**
all have a spiral which goes anti-clockwise;
the spiral of **b** has too thick a line and the spiral of **e** has a hook at the end

9. **a**
all are the same figure, rotated;
all options (apart from **a**) have defects

10. **b**
all have a large shape with white dots, a medium shape with horizontal lines and a grey triangle;
the triangle must overlap the dotted shape

11. **d**
the outer shapes have one more side than the black shape inside them and the inner shape has one less side than the white shape;
the shapes always go black-white-black

12. **c**
all figures contain one more arrow than the number of straight lines
e.g. 2 arrows and 1 line
option **c** has 1 arrow and 0 lines

Section 2

13. **a** MT
first letter = shape e.g. square;
second letter = number of arrowheads

14. **d** RF
first letter = shading e.g. dots;
second letter = thickness of border

15. **c** AU
first letter = direction of arrow;
second letter = pattern in small square

16. **e** PB
first letter = number of black dots;
second letter = number of white dots

17. **b** ML
first letter = number of arrowheads;
second letter = number of lines with no arrowheads;

18. **e** JS
first letter = outer shape e.g. triangle;
second letter = number of divisions e.g. halves or quarters

19. **a** AR
first letter = number of squares which overlap another square;
second letter = number of squares which do not overlap other squares

20. **a** CD
first letter = shading of first ellipse;
second letter = shading of third ellipse

21. **d** YF
first letter = number of straight lines;
second letter = shading of outer shape

22. **a** OS
first letter = number of arrowheads on curved line;
second letter = number of arrowheads on straight line

23. **d** YD
first letter = rotation of small quadrilaterals (either all squares, all rhombuses or mixed);
second letter = number of small shapes odd or even

24. **a** LS
first letter = number of lines of symmetry;
second letter = odd or even number of black stars

Section 3

25. **c** is correct
net **a** has no arrow;
net **b** has the arrow pointing to grey;
net **d** has the arrow pointing to the star;
net **e** has the black face on the right

26. **a** is correct
net **b** has the triangle point towards the line
net **c** has the line on the right, not left;
net **d** has the triangle to the left of the line;
net **e** has the triangle rotated the wrong way

27. **d** is correct
net **a** has the black and half-shaded opposite
net **b** has the half-shaded face rotated 180°;
net **c** has the black face left instead of right;
net **e** has the half-shaded face grey

28. **d** is correct
net **a** has the stripes in the wrong direction;
net **b** has a black circle;
net **c** has the stripes in the wrong direction;
net **e** has the line opposite the circle

29. **e** is correct
net **a** has the circle opposite the arrow;
net **b** has the arrow pointing to the circle;
net **c** has the circle opposite the arrow;
net **d** has the circle to the right of the arrow

30. **b** is correct
net **a** has the diagonal line the wrong way;
net **c** has the line opposite the grey face;
net **d** has the diagonal line the wrong way;
net **e** has the grey face opposite the line

31. **c** is correct
net **a** has the black face to the right;
net **b** has the three squares the wrong way;
net **d** has the squares opposite black;
net **e** has the black face to the right

32. **a** is correct
net **b** has the circle opposite the line;
net **c** has the circle opposite the line;
net **d** has the stripes opposite the line;
net **e** has the line in the wrong direction

33. **b** is correct
net **a** has the star and the cross opposite;
net **c** has the star rotated incorrectly;
net **d** has the pattern rotated;
net **e** has the cross rotated incorrectly

34. **b** is correct
net **a** has the chequers rotated incorrectly;
net **c** has the grey face on the right;
net **d** has no chequers at all;
net **e** has diagonal chequers

35. **d** is correct
net **a** has the dots rotated incorrectly;
net **b** has the dots rotated incorrectly;
net **c** has the dots rotated incorrectly;
net **e** has the dots rotated incorrectly

36. **a** is correct
net **b** has the stripes rotated incorrectly;
net **c** has a flat top to the backwards L;
net **d** has the L shape deformed;
net **e** has the top of the L touching black

NVR Paper 1 cont.

Section 4

37. **d** is correct
arrow must point NE (reflective symmetry);
arrow must match the bottom row style

38. **d** is correct
left shapes are smaller;
middle row is squares;
each row has both stripe directions

39. **e** is correct
must be reflection of bottom left;
style and thickness of dotted line must match the others

40. **b** is correct
each row contains 1, 3 and 5 lines;
direction of lines alternates;
thickness of line must match

41. **b** is correct
top left square is black (so not **d**);
smaller circle towards centre;
position of circles must be symmetrical
(not too close to the white square)

42. **d** is correct
each row and column should contain all three shades of star;
stars on diagonal bottom-left to top-right all have highlight top right;
star **a** is too small

43. **a** is correct
shading must match rectangles above;
border must be in between top and bottom circles; circle must be central

44. **c** is correct
arrow is white;
left figures have 2 straight lines (L shape);
thickness of lines must match bottom row

45. **b** is correct
rotation of shapes must match;
line thickness must match row;
pattern is large dots

46. **a** is correct
lozenge must be central;
lines on top row are horizontal;
spacing of lines must match row

47. **b** is correct
stars have 5, 6, 7 points (L to Right);
each row contains three different shadings;
orientation of star must match row

48. **e** is correct
figure must match bottom row;
rotation must match left column;
lines in circle alternate direction

Maths Paper 2

1. **C** 17
   14 + 3 = 17
   (14 is incorrect as the 3 who played tennis and rounders and athletics have to be included)

2. **D** 2
   $\frac{1}{4} \div \frac{1}{8} = \frac{1}{4} \times \frac{8}{1} = \frac{8}{4} = 2$

3. **B** circle
   a circle has an infinite number of lines of symmetry

4. **B** 18
   at 50mph, 60 miles will take 1 hour (50 miles) plus the time taken for 10 miles (1 hour x $\frac{10}{50}$ = 60mins ÷5 = 12 minutes)
   so if he took 1.5 hours = 90mins and he travelled for (90mins – 1 hour and 12 minutes = 90 – 72 = 18mins)

5. **B** $1500cm^3$
   V = $\pi \times r^2 \times l$ = 3 x 5^2x 20 = 3 x 25 x 20
   ≐ 75 x 20 = 75 x 2 x 10 = 150 x 10 = 1500
   units must match so **D** is incorrect

6. **D** **HEED**
   horizontal line of symmetry

7. **A** 139
   $12^2 - 16 \div 2 + \sqrt[2]{9}$ = 144 – (16 ÷ 2) + 3
   = 144 – 8 + 3 = 136 + 3 = 139

8. **D** 144°
   8 : 3 : 5 : 4 is 360°
   (total of angles in quadrilateral)
   8 + 3 + 5 + 4 = 20
   360 ÷ 20 = 18 (ratios 1)
   largest = 8 x 18 = 80 + 64 = 144

9. **B** £20
   320 = Ellie (1 part),
   Isobel (5 x Ellie = 5 x 1 = 5 parts),
   Danny (2 x Isobel = 2 x 5 = 10 parts)
   There are 16 parts in total.
   320 ÷ 16 = 20 (value of 1 part)
   Ellie gets £20

10. **B** 16:19
    distance = 375km, speed = 150km/h
    time = distance ÷speed = 375 ÷150
    = 37.5 ÷ 15 = 2.5 (two and a half)
    (2 x 15 = 30, half of 15 = 7.5)
    13:49 + 2 hours = 15:49;
    15:49 + 30mins = 16:19

11. **E** 170,000
    10% of 200,000 = 20,000 (charity)
    5% of 200,000 = 20,000 ÷ 2 = 10,000;
    she gives away 20,000 + 10,000 = 30,000;
    she has 200,000 – 30,000 left = 170,000

12. **B** 10mm
    mean = add the amounts and divide by number of amounts (12);
    17 + 14 + 12 + 20 + 12 + 4 + 2 + 1 + 5 + 9 + 10 + 14 = 120;
    120 ÷ 12 = 10

13. **B** 56
    divide the total by 3;
    171 ÷ 3 = 57 (the middle number);
    the three consecutive numbers are:
    56, 57 and 58, smallest is 56

14. **C** $30m^2$
    area of outer rectangle = 12 x 6 = 72;
    area of top left triangle = $\frac{1}{2} \times b \times h$;
    height = 6 – 3 = 3; $\frac{1}{2}$ x 4 x 3 = 6;
    area of lower right triangle = $\frac{1}{2}$ x 12 x 6 = 36
    garden area = 72 – (6 + 36) = 72 – 42 = 30

Maths Paper 2 cont.

15. **B** 32.2 kg

total mass = 7 x 4.6 = (7 x 4) + (7 x 0.6)

= 28 + 4.2 = 32.2

16. **C** 1:2000

number of cm in 3km = 3 x 1000 x 100

= 3000 x 100 = 300, 000;

150cm : 3km = 150:300,000

300,000 ÷ 150 = 30000 ÷ 15 = 2000

so ratio simplifies to 1:2000

17. **E** 132cm

12cm = $2x$; $x = 6$

P = $20x$ + 12 (total of all sides)

= (20 x 6) + 12 = 120 + 12 = 132

18. **E** 0.75

total counters = 9 + 4 + 10 + 13 = 36;

not red = 4 + 10 + 13 = 27;

P(not red) = $\frac{27}{36} = \frac{3}{4}$ = 0.75

19. **B** 10

$6^2 + 4^3$ = 36 + (4 x 4 x 4) = 36 + 64 = 100;

$\sqrt{100}$ = 10

20. **B** 24

100m in 15s = 1km in 150s (x10);

1 hour = 60 x 60 = 3600 seconds;

3600 ÷ 150 = 360 ÷ 15 = 24

1km in 150s = 24km in 3600s (x24)

= 24kph

21. **C** 30

Mon = 18 ÷ 4.5 = 4 cars;

Tue/Fri = 13.5 ÷ 4.5 x 2 = 6 cars;

Wed = 40.5 ÷ 4.5 = 9 cars;

Sat = 49.5 ÷ 4.5 = 11 cars;

total cars = 4 + 6 + 9 + 11 = 30 cars

22. **B** 404

20% = one fifth;

one fifth of 505 = 505 ÷ 5 = 101;

505 – 101 = 404

23. **D** 764.78

24. **D** £56.11

27.99 + 31.4 + 4.5 = 63.89;

120 – 63.89 = 56.11

25. **B** 7.5

50% of 180 = 90;

$\frac{1}{4}$ of 90 = 90 ÷ 4 = (90 ÷ 2) ÷ 2 = 45 ÷ 2 = 22.5

$\frac{1}{3}$ of 22.5 = 22.5 ÷ 3;

225 ÷ 3 = 75; 22.5 ÷ 3 = 7.5

English Paper 2

1. **A** her father died (line 8)
2. **B** pious = religious/devout
3. **B** entranced

   e.g. he was entranced by her beauty
4. **D** William and Henry (lines 26 and 41)
5. **E** named Henry as his choice for king (line 32)
6. **A** tempestuous

   reign was harmonious = peaceful reign;

   reign was tempestuous = turbulent reign
7. **C** he was too immature to rule independently

   wield power = use his power
8. **D** inhibited

   inhibited = withdrawn and subdued
9. **A** it was expected that royal weddings would be elaborate

   unbecoming = inappropriate;

   it would be inappropriate for a royal wedding to be simple and secret
10. **D** John

    her last son (line 49)
11. **E** she cared deeply for her children

    maternal = motherly, kind, tender

    devotion = dedication
12. **E** retreated

    (line 45) *Eleanor retreated to France = Eleanor went back to France*

13. **D** gray

    should be *grey*
14. **A** portraid

    should be *portrayed*
15. **A** connisseur

    should be *connoisseur*
16. **C** opulant

    should be *opulent*
17. **C** geniel

    should be *genial*
18. **C** tirade

    tepid, tiered, tirade, tired, triage
19. **A** corona

    cornet, cornice, corona, coronet, corroborate
20. **D** fricassee

    fraise, fraught, fricassee, friend, frieze
21. **C** invade

    environment, envelop, invade, invincible, invite
22. **C** tenon

    temperature, tempest, tenon, tent, tenuous

23. **B** dubious

    dubious = doubtful

    he did not have a certain claim
24. **E** betrothed

    betrothed = engaged to be married
25. **A** business

    business = running

    e.g. day-to-day running of the government
26. **C** by

    you are imprisoned *by* someone
27. **E** even
28. **A** Although
29. **C** arguably
30. **B** lack

VR Paper 2

Section 1

1. **C** pulse & **Y** legume
pulses and legumes grow in pods

2. **C** bacterial & **X** viral
both are types of infection

3. **A** heavy & **Y** hefty
both mean heavy

4. **C** forgive & **Y** exonerate
exonerate = pardon/forgive

5. **A** deny & **X** repudiate
repudiate = renounce/deny

6. **C** ardent & **Y** keen
both mean *enthusiastic*

7. **B** winsome & **Y** fetching
both are adjectives meaning *attractive*

Section 2

8. **C** liquid
ice is a solid;
milk is a liquid

9. **B** builder
a chef makes biscuits;
a builder makes walls

10. **D** fish
a parliament of owls;
a school of fish
(collective nouns)

11. **E** chronic
concerning = about/relating to;
chronic = returning/repeating
e.g. chronic pain, chronic liar

12. **A** head
impart = convey/communicate
e.g. impart advice
lead = main/head
e.g. he was the head chef

13. **C** retake
you can sign a manuscript
(add *re* to make *resign* = quit)
you can take a walk
(add *re* to make *retake* = resit)

14. **B** representative
technical is an adjective that can describe an expert
i.e. technical expert
political is an adjective that can describe a representative
i.e. political representative (MP)

15. **D** guard
lease+holder = leaseholder
van+guard = vanguard (=forerunner)

16. **E** descendant
rain sounds like *reign = control;*
sun sounds like *son = descendant*

17. **A** Ken
Order: Ronnie, Tina, Ken, Emma, Brian

Section 3

18. **B** 144
each term x2
e.g. 36 = 18 x 2

19. **D** 66
(R to Left) +4, +5, +6, +7, +8;
58 + 8 = 66

20. **B** 350
+75
e.g. 275 + 75 = 350

21. **A** 117
add previous two terms
e.g. 27 + 45 = 72
45 + 72 = 117

22. **C** 64
cube numbers
$4^3 = 4 \times 4 \times 4 = 64$

23. **B** 1

÷ 10

e.g. 1000 ÷ 10 = 100

10 ÷ 10 = 1

24. **A** 5

x3, x4, x5, x6

? x 3 = 15;

15 ÷ 3 = 5

25. **E** 900

+212

688 + 212 = 900

26. **C** 12

+11, +10, +9, +8

? + 11 = 23;

23 – 11 = 12

27. **E** 322

-111, -222, -333

655 – 333 = 322

Section 4

28. **A** KQ

first letter B -> C (+1)

so J -> K (+1);

second letter Z -> Y (-1)

so R -> Q (-1);

JR -> KQ

29. **D** Vt

first letter C -> G (+4)

so R -> V (+4);

second letter f -> e (-1)

so u -> t (-1);

Ru -> Vt

30. **B** IKM

all letters +6

C + 6 = I; E + 6 = K; G + 6 = M

31. **E** PQTU

first two letters fit between second four letters to make alphabetical sequence:

i.e. MN -> KL MN OP -> KLOP

so RS -> PQ RS TU -> PQTU

32. **A** bcd

take repeated letter (*e.g. BB*) and count back five letters (-> *w*) then add following two letters, all three lower case (-> *wxy*)

so GG -> b (-5) -> bcd

33. **B** Ro

first letter of first pair -1 (*i.e. f – 1 = e*) becomes second letter of second pair;

second letter of first pair + 1 (*i.e. H + 1 = I*) becomes first letter of second pair;

cases stay the same (*e.g.* lower -> lower)

pQ -> (Q + 1)(p – 1) = Ro

34. **E** DeG

all letters +7, cases must match

35. **D** Ta

both letters -9 (T ->K and A -> r)

second letter changes from upper to lower case

(*i.e. A -> r, not R)*

CJ -> (C – 9)(J – 9) = Ta

36. **A** jXlP

first letter -2, second letter +2;

third letter -2, fourth letter +2;

cases swap (*e.g. upper -> lower*)

L -> L – 2 = j; v -> v + 2 = X;

N -> N – 2 = l; n -> n + 2 = P;

LvNn -> jXlP

VR Paper 2 cont.

Section 5

37. **B** 7 8 4 1
7487 must be GANG (G first and last);
G = 7, A = 4, N = 8;
1487 must be TANG (ANG = 487); T = 1;
7841 = GNAT

38. **A** G A I N
G = 7, A = 4, N = 8;
7498 = GA?N;
one possible option: GAIN
I = 9

39. **E** 7 9 4 8 1
G = 7, 9 = I, A = 4, N = 8, T = 1

40. **B** 9 7 4 3 2 9
562292 must be CHEESE (position of E);
C = 5, H = 6, E = 2, S = 9;
924356 = SE??CH;
one possible option: SEARCH;
A = 4, R = 3;
SNARES = 9?4329 (only possible option);
N = 7

41. **C** S O O N E R
9 = S, 88 = ??, 7 = N, 2 = E, 3 = R;
only possible option is SOONER;
O = 8

42. **E** 5 6 4 9 2 3 9
C = 5, H = 6, A = 4, S = 9, E = 2, R = 3, S = 9

Section 6

43. **C** S A T E D
SATED -> DATES
link is fruit

44. **D** S H O R E
SHORE -> HORSE
link is animals

45. **A** B R E A K
BREAK -> BAKER;
link is professions

46. **B** G R O A N
GROAN -> ORGAN;
link is the body

47. **C** S L I M E
SLIME -> MILES;
link is measurement

48. **E** D R A W E R
DRAWER -> REWARD;
link is winning

49. **A** D I C E R
DICER -> CRIED;
link is tears

50. **A** S O F T E R
SOFTER -> FOREST;
link is trees

51. **D** W I R E D
WIRED -> WIDER;
link is comparatives

52. **D** Ellie has a wooden jewellery box
oak = wood -> wooden box;
cannot infer any other statement

Section 7

53. **A** sing
54. **D** paws
55. **E** pass
56. **B** vine
57. **A** gone
58. **D** meld
59. **A** heat
60. **A** pose

Section 8

61. **C** happy & **E** content
malicious, unkind and *cruel* are all adjectives which mean *nasty*;
happy and *content* mean *satisfied*

62. **A** assist & **D** basket
hamper, hinder and *impede* are all verbs which mean *delay* or *obstruct*

63. **B** dwelling & **C** home
reside, inhabit and *live* are all verbs which mean *dwell*;
dwelling and *home* are nouns which are the name of a place to live

64. **A** apiary & **E** influenza
apathy, contentment and *influence* are all abstract nouns;
apiary (beehive) and *influenza (flu)* are common nouns

65. **B** refuse & **C** royalty
accessory, regalia and *accoutrement* are all nouns meaning *extra* or *trimmings*

66. **A** create & **D** build
demolish, annihilate and *raze (flatten)* are all verbs which mean *to destroy* in some way
create & *build* are verbs meaning *to make*

67. **C** homely & *relinquish*
earthquake, upstream and *grasshopper* are all compound words (*earth+quake, up+stream, grass+hopper*) whereas *homely* and *relinquish* are not

68. **B** wine & **C** star
port, liner and *anchor* are all terms to do with boats or ships whereas *wine* and *star* are not

Section 9

69. **B** NQZMFD
each letter -1
e.g. P -> O, E -> D;
O -> N, R -> Q, etc.

70. **D** TVDVYRPVP
+1, +2, +3...
e.g. S -> T (+1); T -> V (+2)...
STAR = TVDV;
T -> Y (+5); L -> R (+6)...

71. **A** BQKNAC
-2, +2, -3, +3, -4...
D -> B (-2); O -> Q (+2); N -> K (-3)...

72. **C** PLANE
+1, -2, +3, -4...
inverse: -1, +2, -3, +4...
Q – 1 = P; J + 2 = L; D – 3 = A;
J + 4 = N; J – 5 = E;
QJDJJ -> PLANE

73. **A** NIGHT
-1, +2, -3, +4...
inverse: +1, -2, +3, -4...
M + 1 = N; K – 2 = I; D + 3 = G;
L – 4 = H; O + 5 = T;
MKDLO -> NIGHT

Section 10

74. **B** 9
55 ÷ 5 = 11; 90 ÷ 10 = 9

75. **C** 43
2 x 12 + 1 = 25; 6 x 7 + 1 = 43

76. **D** 35
17 + 3 = 20; 20 + 3 = 23;
27 + 4 = 31; 31 + 4 = 35

77. **E** 35
8 x 8 ÷ 2 = 32; 7 x 10 ÷ 2 = 35

78. **B**
(90 – 18) x 2 = 144; (75 – 55) x 2 = 40

79. **A** 11
100 ÷ 25 + 1 = 5; 200 ÷ 20 + 1 = 11

80. **B** 7
2 x 100 ÷ 5 = 40; 7 x 5 ÷ 5 = 7

NVR Paper 2

Section 1

1. b
2. e
3. c
4. d
5. d
6. c
7. d
8. a
9. b
10. a
11. b
12. c

Section 2

13. c
14. d
15. a
16. b
17. d
18. c
19. e
20. b
21. a
22. b
23. e
24. d

Section 3

25. **c**
circle gets bigger;
outline gets thicker;
arrow rotates 45°;
arrow stays same size

26. **a**
number of black stars decreases by 1;
number of grey squares increases by 1;
stars overlap squares
(not the other way round);
stars stay the same size

27. **e**
circle stays the same size;
circle shading gets lighter;
line has black triangle;
triangle increases in size;
circle outline does not change

28. **a**
number of stars inside rectangle +1;
arrow gets thinner;
arrow must point to a star

29. **c**
black circle rotates anti-clockwise around the points of the star;
inner ellipse gets darker;
ellipse does not rotate;
inner circle moves left to right

30. **b**
number of line crossings increases by 1;
number of sides of shape increases by 1

31. **d**
whole shape and shadings rotate anti-clockwise by 72°

32. **b**
lines and shapes figure rotates 90° clockwise;
order of shapes rotates
i.e. (anti-clockwise) circle-triangle-square -> triangle-square-circle -> square-circle-triangle etc.;
middle of three shapes is always black, outers are always white;
stripes in separate triangle alternate horizontal-vertical-horizontal...

33. **c**
sock shape shading becomes finer;
length of line gets shorter;
must have circle

34. **d**
position of T-shape rotates clockwise;
shading alternates white-black-white...
length of T-shape increases;
T-shape must be central (so not **C**)

35. **b**
number of points on shape increases by 1;
lines inside shape get closer together
lines rotate in direction

36. **b**
number of arrowheads increases by 1;
must be one crossing point only

Section 4

37. **a**
whole figure rotates anti-clockwise 90°;
border of triangle must stay the same

38. **c**
up arrows change to down arrows;
down arrows stay as down arrows

39. **e**
line is reflected horizontally;
circles and squares are switched and reflected
i.e. three squares top left ->
three circles top right

40. **b**
grey shading -> patterned;
patterned -> black
(star and rectangle shading);
line stays same thickness;
ends of line touching star -> arrows;
ends of line through rectangle -> squares

41. **d**
black shading -> white;
white shading -> grey;
grey shading -> black
number of stars stays the same;
number of squares stays the same

42. **b**
figure rotates 180°;
arrow changes from black to grey;
shading of triangle black -> grey

43. **c**
circle gets smaller;
arrow gets thinner and lighter;
rectangle outline -> grey;

44. **e**
shading of ellipse does not change;
arrowheads stay the same;
shape rotates 90° anti-clockwise;

45. **b**
three separate pieces merge into one;
sizes do not change

46. **c**
outer shape becomes inner shape;
inner shape becomes outer shape;
fill pattern rotated 180°

47. **b**
plain arrow head with wings -> reflected;
arrow with two Vs – only the Vs reversed;
arrow with two part head – swap colours

48. **e**
if shapes are ordered, they show the order of shading needed for the large shape with smaller shapes inside it;
*i.e. shading of pentagons in order from largest to smallest = shading of shapes in option **e** from largest to smallest: grey, white, dark grey, white, black*

TEST ADMINISTRATION

AND MARKING

Administering the Tests

These tests are designed to give your child valuable practice for the tests which they will sit (usually in September). It is recommended that they have a quiet place to work, where they won't be disturbed. It would also be very useful for them to have a clock or timer so that they can judge how much time they have.

There are three tests: a maths test, and English test and a reasoning test. There is also a writing test which is not marked but may be used as evidence in borderline cases. This book contains two different examples of each test. Your child can either begin with maths test 1 and proceed through the tests in order or it is also possible to mix and match tests from the first half and the second half of this book.

Equipment needed for the tests is just this book and a pen or pencil. Answers can be written straight into the book or (for a more authentic mock test) you can download a separate answer sheet, similar to the one in the real test. Visit *www.kemsingtuition.co.uk/elevenplus2019* to get this free resource.

There are clear instructions at the bottom of pages and at the end of sections, explaining whether to continue or wait. You should make your child aware of these before each of the tests.

Maths and English Test – 1 hour
Go through the maths practice questions with your child and tell them that when they begin, they will have 25 minutes to complete the test. They should answer all of the questions, even if they have to guess when running out of time at the end. They should answer as quickly as they can. The design of this book includes lots of space for working out answers, including intentional blank pages to prevent your child from seeing the next section too early. They should be encouraged to use these spaces. However only the recorded answer will be marked, and no credit can be given for answers elsewhere.

Following the maths test, they should have a short break and then (with your help) complete the English practice questions. The procedure is then similar to the maths test. In both parts of this test, you can give them a warning when their time is nearly up.

Reasoning Test – 1 hour

The reasoning test is in two parts: verbal reasoning and non-verbal reasoning (which includes spatial reasoning). In the actual test, your child may be given a short timed practice. This element is not included in this book.

There are 80 verbal reasoning questions and a time limit of 30 minutes. Your child should be encouraged to work quickly and to read the questions and examples carefully, before working their way through all sections of the test on their own. This time, you do not help them with the example questions.

The second part to this test, non-verbal and spatial, is in four sections. You should go through the example for the first section and then allow 6 minutes for your child to complete all 12 questions. The actual test may have less questions and less time, but 30 seconds per question is usual. After the first section is complete, do the same for the other sections. Once your child has moved on to the next section, they cannot go back and change anything in a previous section.

Writing Test – 40 minutes

You may need extra paper for the writing test, although there is space in this book if it will fit. Read through the question with your child and then give them ten minutes to plan their writing. After ten minutes they should begin.

Marking the Tests

When all tests are complete, check the answers and then add up the number correct to get a raw score. Then go to the following section to work out a standardised score.

Interpreting the Scores

Disclaimer
These tests have been carefully compiled to prepare your child for the real test. However, they are not the real test and performance in these tests should only be used as a guide. Poor performance in these tests does not necessarily mean your child will fail in the actual test but will show you which areas they need to work on. Good performance in these tests is a good indicator that your child will do well in the actual tests, but there is no guarantee – nerves on the day can affect scores. Knowing what to expect though, is a good way to combat those nerves.

Standardisation
The raw scores (the actual number of questions correct) will be converted into a standardised score when the actual test is marked. This score is calculated using a number of factors such as age of the child, how difficult the test is and the number of questions asked. For this reason, each year the standardisation process is slightly different. The look-up tables which follow are a guide for you to assess how well your child is doing but are not the ones that will actually be used in the real thing.

When you receive your child's eleven plus results, you will be told what the pass mark is. This may change slightly from year to year and so will not necessarily match the pass mark in these mock tests.

To 'pass' this mock test, your child needs to score a total of 323 out of a total of 141. It is not possible to score more than 141 (or less than 69) on any test. In addition to scoring 323 or more, your child also needs to score no less than 107 marks in any individual test. If their score is in the grey region on the table, then they have not attained this.

Mathematics Test – interpretation of scores

Maths	10y 0m	10y 1m	10y 2m	10y 3m	10y 4m	10y 5m	10y 6m	10y 7m	10y 8m	10y 9m	10y 10m	10y 11m	10y 12m	11y 0m
0	91	87	83	80	76	73	69	69	69	69	69	69	69	69
1	94	91	87	83	80	76	73	69	69	69	69	69	69	69
2	98	94	91	87	83	80	76	73	69	69	69	69	69	69
3	101	98	94	91	87	83	80	76	73	69	69	69	69	69
4	105	101	98	94	91	87	83	80	76	73	69	69	69	69
5	109	105	101	98	94	91	87	83	80	76	73	69	69	69
6	112	109	105	101	98	94	91	87	83	80	76	73	69	69
7	116	112	109	105	101	98	94	91	87	83	80	76	73	69
8	119	116	112	109	105	101	98	94	91	87	83	80	76	73
9	123	119	116	112	109	105	101	98	94	91	87	83	80	76
10	127	123	119	116	112	109	105	101	98	94	91	87	83	80
11	130	127	123	119	116	112	109	105	101	98	94	91	87	83
12	134	130	127	123	119	116	112	109	105	101	98	94	91	87
13	137	134	130	127	123	119	116	112	109	105	101	98	94	91
14	141	137	134	130	127	123	119	116	112	109	105	101	98	94
15	141	141	137	134	130	127	123	119	116	112	109	105	101	98
16	141	141	141	137	134	130	127	123	119	116	112	109	105	101
17	141	141	141	141	137	134	130	127	123	119	116	112	109	105
18	141	141	141	141	141	137	134	130	127	123	119	116	112	109
19	141	141	141	141	141	141	137	134	130	127	123	119	116	112
20	141	141	141	141	141	141	141	137	134	130	127	123	119	116
21	141	141	141	141	141	141	141	141	137	134	130	127	123	119
22	141	141	141	141	141	141	141	141	141	137	134	130	127	123
23	141	141	141	141	141	141	141	141	141	141	137	134	130	127
24	141	141	141	141	141	141	141	141	141	141	141	137	134	130
25	141	141	141	141	141	141	141	141	141	141	141	141	137	134

Instructions

Work out your child's age (in years and months) and add up their score from the test.

Find their score on the left hand side and then read off their standardised score in the column for their age. Younger children are given a higher standardised score for achieving the same number of correct answers as they are less experienced.

English Test – interpretation of scores

English	10y 0m	10y 1m	10y 2m	10y 3m	10y 4m	10y 5m	10y 6m	10y 7m	10y 8m	10y 9m	10y 10m	10y 11m	10y 12m	11y 0m
0	88	85	82	79	75	72	69	69	69	69	69	69	69	69
1	91	88	85	82	79	75	72	69	69	69	69	69	69	69
2	95	91	88	85	82	79	75	72	69	69	69	69	69	69
3	98	95	91	88	85	82	79	75	72	69	69	69	69	69
4	101	98	95	91	88	85	82	79	75	72	69	69	69	69
5	104	101	98	95	91	88	85	82	79	75	72	69	69	69
6	107	104	101	98	95	91	88	85	82	79	75	72	69	69
7	111	107	104	101	98	95	91	88	85	82	79	75	72	69
8	114	111	107	104	101	98	95	91	88	85	82	79	75	72
9	117	114	111	107	104	101	98	95	91	88	85	82	79	75
10	120	117	114	111	107	104	101	98	95	91	88	85	82	79
11	123	120	117	114	111	107	104	101	98	95	91	88	85	82
12	127	123	120	117	114	111	107	104	101	98	95	91	88	85
13	130	127	123	120	117	114	111	107	104	101	98	95	91	88
14	133	130	127	123	120	117	114	111	107	104	101	98	95	91
15	136	133	130	127	123	120	117	114	111	107	104	101	98	95
16	139	136	133	130	127	123	120	117	114	111	107	104	101	98
17	141	139	136	133	130	127	123	120	117	114	111	107	104	101
18	141	141	139	136	133	130	127	123	120	117	114	111	107	104
19	141	141	141	139	136	133	130	127	123	120	117	114	111	107
20	141	141	141	141	139	136	133	130	127	123	120	117	114	111
21	141	141	141	141	141	139	136	133	130	127	123	120	117	114
22	141	141	141	141	141	141	139	136	133	130	127	123	120	117
23	141	141	141	141	141	141	141	139	136	133	130	127	123	120
24	141	141	141	141	141	141	141	141	139	136	133	130	127	123
25	141	141	141	141	141	141	141	141	141	139	136	133	130	127
26	141	141	141	141	141	141	141	141	141	141	139	136	133	130
27	141	141	141	141	141	141	141	141	141	141	141	139	136	133
28	141	141	141	141	141	141	141	141	141	141	141	141	139	136
29	141	141	141	141	141	141	141	141	141	141	141	141	141	139
30	141	141	141	141	141	141	141	141	141	141	141	141	141	141

Reasoning Test – interpretation of scores

Reasoning	10y 0m	10y 1m	10y 2m	10y 3m	10y 4m	10y 5m	10y 6m	10y 7m	10y 8m	10y 9m	10y 10m	10y 11m	10y 12m	11y 0m
0 - 5	91	87	83	80	76	73	69	69	69	69	69	69	69	69
6 - 10	94	91	87	83	80	76	73	69	69	69	69	69	69	69
11 - 15	98	94	91	87	83	80	76	73	69	69	69	69	69	69
16 - 20	101	98	94	91	87	83	80	76	73	69	69	69	69	69
21 - 25	105	101	98	94	91	87	83	80	76	73	69	69	69	69
26 - 30	109	105	101	98	94	91	87	83	80	76	73	69	69	69
31 - 35	112	109	105	101	98	94	91	87	83	80	76	73	69	69
36 - 40	116	112	109	105	101	98	94	91	87	83	80	76	73	69
41 - 45	119	116	112	109	105	101	98	94	91	87	83	80	76	73
46 - 50	123	119	116	112	109	105	101	98	94	91	87	83	80	76
51 - 55	127	123	119	116	112	109	105	101	98	94	91	87	83	80
56 - 60	130	127	123	119	116	112	109	105	101	98	94	91	87	83
61 - 65	134	130	127	123	119	116	112	109	105	101	98	94	91	87
66 - 70	137	134	130	127	123	119	116	112	109	105	101	98	94	91
71 - 75	141	137	134	130	127	123	119	116	112	109	105	101	98	94
76 - 80	141	141	137	134	130	127	123	119	116	112	109	105	101	98
81 - 85	141	141	141	137	134	130	127	123	119	116	112	109	105	101
86 - 90	141	141	141	141	137	134	130	127	123	119	116	112	109	105
91 - 95	141	141	141	141	141	137	134	130	127	123	119	116	112	109
96 - 100	141	141	141	141	141	141	137	134	130	127	123	119	116	112
101 - 105	141	141	141	141	141	141	141	137	134	130	127	123	119	116
106 - 110	141	141	141	141	141	141	141	141	137	134	130	127	123	119
111 - 115	141	141	141	141	141	141	141	141	141	137	134	130	127	123
115 - 119	141	141	141	141	141	141	141	141	141	141	137	134	130	127
120 - 124	141	141	141	141	141	141	141	141	141	141	141	137	134	130
125 +	141	141	141	141	141	141	141	141	141	141	141	141	137	134

Instructions

Work out your child's age (in years and months) and add up their score from the test.

Find their score band on the left-hand side and then read off their standardised score in the column for their age. Younger children are given a higher standardised score for achieving the same number of correct answers as they are less experienced.

Thank you for buying this book – I hope that you found it useful. Everything has been checked and double checked to eliminate any errors. However, it is possible that one has been missed somewhere. If you happen to find it, please email

richard@kemsingtuition.co.uk

with full details of the error and the page on which you found it. If you are the first person to report the error, and you include your name and address, then you will be sent a copy of the next edition of the book with any errors corrected.

Printed in Great Britain
by Amazon

42127394R00142